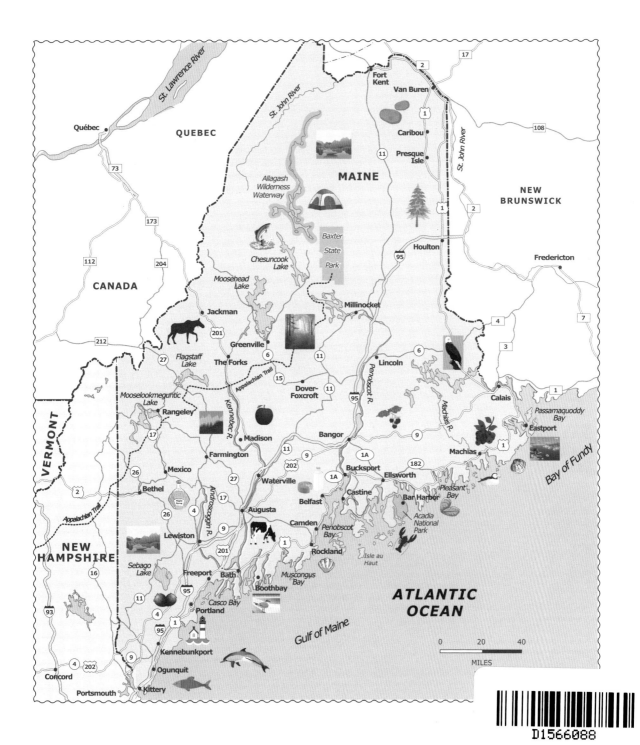

MAINE

QUEBEC

St. Lawrence River

Québec

CANADA

VERMONT

NEW
HAMPSHIRE

St. John River

Fort
Kent

Van Buren

Caribou

Presque
Isle

Allagash
Wilderness
Waterway

Chesuncook
Lake

Moosehead
Lake

Baxter
State
Park

Jackman

Greenville

The Forks

Flagstaff
Lake

Mooselookmeguntic
Lake

Rangeley

Madison

Farmington

Mexico

Bethel

Lewiston

Sebago
Lake

Freeport

Bath

Portland

Kennebunkport

Ogunquit

Kittery

Portsmouth

Concord

Millinocket

Dover-
Foxcroft

Lincoln

Bangor

Waterville

Augusta

Camden

Rockland

Boothbay

Houlton

Calais

Eastport

Machias

Ellsworth

Bucksport

Belfast

Castine

Bar Harbor

Acadia
National
Park

Fredericton

NEW
BRUNSWICK

St. John River

Passamaquoddy
Bay

Pleasant
Bay

Bay of Fundy

ATLANTIC
OCEAN

Gulf of Maine

Penobscot
Bay

Muscongus
Bay

Isle au
Haut

Casco Bay

Kennebec R.

Androscoggin R.

Penobscot R.

Machias R.

Appalachian Trail

Appalachian Trail

73

212

173

112

204

201

27

6

15

11

11

11

11

9

9

9

9

9

17

17

17

17

26

26

4

4

4

4

1

1

1

1

1

1

1

1A

1A

2

2

2

2

3

4

7

108

17

95

95

95

95

95

182

202

202

201

16

93

MILES

0   20   40

D1566088

New England Summertime Cooking

Sherri Eldridge

Harvest
Hill
p r e s s
Salisbury Cove, Maine

New England Summertime Cooking
by Sherri Eldridge

Published by Harvest Hill Press
P.O. Box 55, Salisbury Cove, Maine 04672

ISBN: 978-1-886862-52-4

First Printing: July 2007

Photography copyrights and credits are listed on page 185

Cover and Text Design and Layout: Sherri Eldridge
Editing: Bill Eldridge, Brenda Koplin, Jerry Goldberg, Fran Goldberg and Joe Fazio

Library of Congress Control Number: 2007922483

Printed on paper manufactured under International Environmental Management
Standard ISO 14001:2004, using Elemental Chlorine Free (ECF) pulps from
sustainable well-managed forests. ISO14001 specifies requirements for an
environmental management system encompassing all environmental aspects over
which a manufacturer has control and can be expected to influence. Elementally
chlorine-free woodpulps are bleached without the use of chlorine gas, a product
found to cause toxins in pulp mill effluents. Compliance with these standards has
been verified by an independent auditor.

Printed in South Korea

This book is dedicated with love to my mother
Fran Goldberg,
who for many years did all her cooking with
three little girls perched on chairs around her.

And to my father,
Jerry Goldberg,
who has loved everything my mother ever made,
and exuberantly conveyed the gift of appreciation.

The New England Cookbook collection follows the American Heart Association Guidelines for Healthy Adults. These wonderful recipes will help make following the American Heart Association guidelines easier and more fun for you by supplying flavorful reduced fat/salt menu ideas using ingredients from your shelves.

...Beth Davis, R.D. M.Ed.

Beth Davis is a registered dietician, former member of the American Heart Association's Speaker's Bureau, and Heart Health Education of the Young Task Force.

The gratitude of the author is extended to the Maine Chapter of the American Heart Association for their guidance, and use of the Association's name to convey the goals of this book. The publisher contributes to the American Heart Association to further its life-preserving efforts of research, outreach and education.

Front Cover: Braised Scallops, page 97; Peach Pie, page 155; Lupin flowers;
Blueberry Muffins, page 31; Fresh Corn, page 135; Tomato Salad, page 72;
Wild Blueberries, page 30; Lobster Bake, page 102; Boston Light on Brewster Island
in Boston Harbor; Common loon; Lemon Cheesecake with Blueberry Topping, page 166.

Back Cover, clockwise from upper left: Newport Harbor Lobster Stew, page 93;
Portland Head Light, Cape Elizabeth, Maine; Zucchini and Shrimp Risotto, page 123;
Steamed Lobster, page 101; Almond Crab Soufflé, page 51; Wild Blueberry Pie, page 152;
Lobster Quiche Tarts, page 45; Raspberries, page 12; Poached Salmon with Dill Sauce, page 109;
Lake Champlain, Vermont; Apricot Fruit Dip, page 60; White Mountains, New Hampshire;
Brandied Peach Preserves, page 171; Apple-Raisin Cole Slaw, page 63.

Bill and Sherri Eldridge on the Great Head trail in Acadia National Park, 2006

Bill is my rock. He takes care of me when I'm writing, obsessing over photos, or buried under piles of paperwork. Bill sets the pace, even on days when it feels like I don't have one. He can be infinitely kind, and equally challenging (although the latter has been said of his wife, too). Bill does most of the cooking in our house, so I do most of the sampling. He is a meticulous cook, my style is more creative. We both have very specific ideas on how to prepare food; and regardless of who's ruling the kitchen, we both end up eating pretty well and feeling quite happy.

Preface

The magnificent harvests of summer spark the imagination of everyone, especially those who love to cook, and all of us who love to eat! This cookbook presents a variety of seasonally fresh recipes, borne of New England fruits, vegetables, and gifts from the sea. There are summertime traditions for festive gatherings, and quick and cool preparations suitable for taking to the beach or setting outside on a buffet. Whatever your calendar holds, please include New England's rich array of tempting recipes.

The American Heart Association has developed sound guidelines to assist in the prevention of heart disease, provides numerous health benefits, and fosters a long and happy life. Traditional recipes have been adapted to meet the guidelines of the American Heart Association for healthy adults, including nutritional analyses to help track your dietary goals. Although reduced in fat, saturated fat and cholesterol, richer treats should be enjoyed just once or twice a week. The recipes in this book are built around a heart-healthy diet which includes a diverse selection of fresh produce, whole grains, fish, nuts, calcium-rich dairy, and very pleasurable food. It is also important to prepare balanced meal plans, offer servings in average size portions, and engage in regular exercise. More information on the American Heart Association's recommendations are listed on page 180.

The recipes in this book are essentially the same as those in *Coastal New England Summertime Cooking.* The new theme represents all of New England's culinary culture, with photographs added to tell their own story of the glorious season, and the delights of vegetarian and seafood cuisines.

Table of Contents

Breakfast and Fruit.................................8

Baked Goods.................................26

Appetizers and Finger Food.....................44

Fresh Greens and Salads.......................62

Soups, Stews and Chowders....................76

Main Meal Dishes..............................94

Pasta, Beans and Grains.......................114

Vegetables and Sauces........................130

Desserts.......................................148

Seasonal Preserves and Jams.................168

Resources and References.....................180

Index...186

Breakfast and Fruit

Whipped Apricot Cream................................9

Cherry-Glazed Fruit................................10

Strawberry-Rhubarb Compote........................11

Raspberry Melon Salad.............................13

Bill's Blueberry Pancakes.........................14

Blueberry Maple Syrup.............................14

Whole Grain Hotcakes..............................15

Real Apple Butter.................................15

Fresh Cherry Crepes...............................16

Vanilla Pecan Waffles.............................18

French Toast......................................19

Raspberry Sauce...................................19

Eggs Benedict Florentine..........................20

Asparagus and Crab Omelette.......................21

Baked Blueberry Porridge..........................23

Crispy Breakfast Potatoes.........................24

Great Granola.....................................25

Whipped Apricot Cream

A lovely way to start the day.

8 fresh apricots

1 cup fresh melon

1 banana, sliced

½ teaspoon lemon juice

½ cup honey

2 cups nonfat plain yogurt

Serves 4

Poach apricots for 5 minutes in boiling water. Drain and cool. Skin, pit and chop poached apricots.

Toss apricots with melon, banana and lemon juice. Chill 20 minutes. Process all ingredients in blender until smooth. Serve with granola and berries.

Serving: 1/4 recipe	Calories: 252	Protein: 7 gm	Fat Calories: 5
Total Fat: 0.5 gm	Dietary Fiber: 2 gm	Sat. Fat: 0 gm	Carbs: 59 gm
Sodium: 90 mg	Fat Component: 2%	Cholesterol: 2 mg	Calcium: 218 mg

Cherry-Glazed Fruit

Sweet and simple – for breakfast or dessert.

1 cup pitted and halved
   fresh or canned cherries

1 tablespoon sugar

6 fresh apples and/or pears

Serves 4

For glaze, process cherries and sugar in blender.

Peel and core apples or pears. Cut vertically into wedges to show shape. Arrange fruit on 4 individual ovenproof dessert plates. Bake 15 minutes at 350º. Remove from oven and drizzle glaze over baked fruit. Serve at once.

Serving: 1/4 recipe	Calories: 217	Protein: 1 gm	Fat Calories: 0
Total Fat: 0 gm	Dietary Fiber: 6 gm	Sat. Fat: 0 gm	Carbs: 53 gm
Sodium: 41 mg	Fat Component: 0%	Cholesterol: 3 mg	Calcium: 26 mg

Strawberry-Rhubarb Compote

Make this the night before. You'll love waking up to this layered delight.

1 cup finely chopped
   rhubarb
3 tablespoons honey
3 tablespoons sugar
½ teaspoon lemon juice
2 cups diced strawberries

Serves 4

Place rhubarb in saucepan with honey, sugar and lemon juice. Simmer over medium heat 15 minutes, or until rhubarb is tender and sauce thickens. Add strawberries to sauce, cook 5 minutes more. Cool a little before serving over pancakes or waffles.

For layered yogurt parfaits, cool compote to room temperature. Chill parfaits before serving.

Serving: 1/2 cup	Calories: 196	Protein: 1 gm	Fat Calories: 0
Total Fat: 0 gm	Dietary Fiber: 2 gm	Sat. Fat: 0 gm	Carbs: 24 gm
Sodium: 2 mg	Fat Component: 0%	Cholesterol: 0 mg	Calcium: 28 mg

Raspberries

Colorful raspberry varieties are summer's fleeting delicacy. The plants grow happily in cold climates, and set new canes each year. Many cultivars produce both summer and fall crops. Fresh raspberries can be combined in recipes with other fresh fruits, or frozen for future use in prepared recipes.

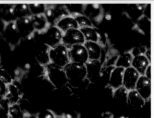

Raspberry Melon Salad

A vibrant palette of summery sweetness.

1 cup fresh raspberries

1 cup fresh blueberries

1 cantaloupe, honeydew
   or catawba melon

2 limes

½ cup sugar

1 teaspoon cornstarch

2 mint leaves, finely chopped

¼ cup chopped pecans

Serves 4

Chill raspberries, blueberries and melon. In a small saucepan, grate 1 tablespoon zest from lime rind, and squeeze juice from both limes. Whisk in sugar and cornstarch, cook over medium heat until mixture starts to thicken. Mix in mint. Remove from heat and cool to room temperature. Cut melon into bite-size pieces. Combine fruit in a large bowl, pour on sauce. Toss lightly with pecans. Chill until served.

Serving: 1/4 recipe	Calories: 175	Protein: 2 gm	Fat Calories: 45
Total Fat: 5 gm	Dietary Fiber: 2 gm	Sat. Fat: 0.5 gm	Carbs: 35 gm
Sodium: 16 mg	Fat Component: 26%	Cholesterol: 0 mg	Calcium: 28 mg

A rookie raspberry-and-melon consumer polishes off the fresh fruit salad with a floral dessert.

Bill's Blueberry Pancakes

Loaded with blueberries!

Serves 4

2 cups flour

1 tablespoon baking powder

2 tablespoons sugar

2 eggs

1½ tablespoons canola oil

2 cups nonfat buttermilk

1½ cups wild blueberries

Sift together dry ingredients. In a separate bowl, beat eggs, then mix in oil and buttermilk. Briefly stir the dry mixture into the liquid, just until combined.

If fresh blueberries are not available, drain canned or defrost frozen blueberries in a sieve (reserve juice for Blueberry Maple Syrup). Fold blueberries into batter, cook at once in nonstick pan.

Serving: 1/4 recipe	Calories: 405	Protein: 14 gm	Fat Calories: 58
Total Fat: 6.5 gm	Dietary Fiber: 3 gm	Sat. Fat: 1.5 gm	Carbs: 68 gm
Sodium: 365 mg	Fat Component: 14%	Cholesterol: 110 mg	Calcium: 299 mg

For pancakes and hotcakes, mix the batter just enough to moisten
the dry ingredients. Some lumps will remain, but just ignore them;
they'll break up during the cooking process.

Blueberry Maple Syrup

Real maple syrup is without equal, please avoid the fake stuff!

Makes 1¼ cups

1 cup maple syrup

½ cup juice pressed or
    drained from blueberries

Combine maple syrup and blueberry juice in medium saucepan. Rapidly boil down over medium-high heat for 25 minutes, or until desired consistency.

Serving: 2 tablespoons	Calories: 84	Protein: 0 gm	Fat Calories: 0
Total Fat: 0 gm	Dietary Fiber: 0 gm	Sat. Fat: 0 gm	Carbs: 22 gm
Sodium: 5 mg	Fat Component: 0%	Cholesterol: 0 mg	Calcium: 33 mg

Whole Grain Hotcakes

Healthy, tasty and fluffy pancakes.

Serves 4

1 cup white whole wheat
  flour *(see note on page 36)*

1 teaspoon baking soda

½ cup finely milled rye or
  buckwheat flour

1 egg

2 tablespoons honey

2 cups nonfat buttermilk

2 tablespoons canola oil

Sift dry ingredients into a large bowl. In a separate bowl, whisk liquid ingredients. Briefly stir dry mixture into the liquid mixture Cook on preheated nonstick lightly greased griddle.

Serving: 1/4 recipe	Calories: 298	Protein: 12 gm	Fat Calories: 54
Total Fat: 6 gm	Dietary Fiber: 4 gm	Sat. Fat: 1 gm	Carbs: 51 gm
Sodium: 151 mg	Fat Component: 18%	Cholesterol: 2 mg	Calcium: 253 mg

Test the heat of the pan by dropping a few drops of water on it.
When the temperature is right, the droplets will bounce and sputter.
If they boil, the pan is too cold. If they immediately vanish, it's too hot.

Real Apple Butter

Melt-in-your mouth apple butter!

Serves 4

2 apples, peeled and grated

½ teaspoon lemon juice

1 tablespoon honey

½ cup powdered sugar

1 cup unsalted whipped
  butter, softened

Press liquid from grated apples. Mix lemon juice and honey into apples. Sift powdered sugar over butter, whip until smooth. Blend mixtures together.

Serving: 1 tablespoon	Calories: 39	Protein: 0 gm	Fat Calories: 36
Total Fat: 4 gm	Dietary Fiber: 0 gm	Sat. Fat: 2 gm	Carbs: 2 gm
Sodium: 1 mg	Fat Component: 92%	Cholesterol: 10 mg	Calcium: 2 mg

Fresh Cherry Crepes

Keep crepes warm in 300° oven until ready to serve.

2 cups unbleached flour

1½ cups skim milk

1½ cups cold water

4 large eggs

2 tablespoons canola oil

2 cups fresh pitted and
    quartered cherries

½ cup sugar

2 teaspoons cornstarch

2 tablespoons water

½ teaspoon vanilla

1 tablespoon Cherry
    Heering or Crème de
    Cassis liqueur (optional)

Makes 8 crepes

Sift flour before measuring into mixing bowl. Slowly whisk milk and water into flour until perfectly smooth, then eggs and oil. Cover and chill 30-60 minutes.

Simmer cherries and sugar in covered saucepan for 15 minutes. Add sugar if needed. In a small bowl, blend cornstarch and water, then stir into cherries. Reduce heat to low, stirring frequently until thickened. Add vanilla and liqueur. Keep warm.

Preheat nonstick crepe pan on medium heat. Grease, then ladle ½ cup batter to middle of pan, quickly tilt to spread. Crepe will be set in 30 seconds. Flip, and cook 20 seconds on second side. Fill each crepe with 2 tablespoons of cherry mixture, and roll.

Serving: 1 crepe	Calories: 267	Protein: 8 gm	Fat Calories: 54
Total Fat: 6 gm	Dietary Fiber: 2 gm	Sat. Fat: 1 gm	Carbs: 45 gm
Sodium: 60 mg	Fat Component: 20%	Cholesterol: 108 mg	Calcium: 79 mg

For a pretty presentation,
dust with powdered sugar,
or cinnamon and sugar.

Eastern Tiger Swallowtail

Clouded Sulphur

Silver-Bordered Fritillary

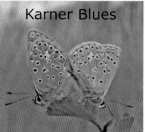

Karner Blues

Most butterflies overwinter as eggs or pupae, but in southern New England some remain as full adults. The Monarchs of summer will migrate to Mexico.

New England Butterflies and Hummingbirds

Question Mark

Ruby-Throated Hummingbirds are resident in all New England areas from May to September. These shimmering little beauties have emerald backs, and males a vibrant ruby throat. They often nest by gardens with continuous summer blooms, drinking from flowers of all shapes and colors.

Silvery Blue

Male

Ruby-Throated Hummingbird

Female

Vanilla Pecan Waffles

Top with warmed maple syrup, fruit sauce or compote.

1¾ cups cake flour

1 tablespoon baking powder

1 tablespoon sugar

2 eggs

1 egg white

3 tablespoons canola oil

1½ cups skim milk

1 teaspoon vanilla

¼ finely chopped pecans

Serves 4

Preheat nonstick waffle iron. Sift flour, baking powder and sugar into a large mixing bowl.

Separate eggs, putting yolks into a medium bowl, and the 3 whites into a small metal bowl. Whip oil into yolks, then milk and vanilla. Beat egg whites until stiff peaks form. Pour yolk mixture into flour, stir briefly. Gently fold in egg whites and pecans.

Ladle batter into waffle iron, cooking until lightly golden. Lightly oil waffle iron between batches.

Serving: 1/4 recipe	Calories: 326	Protein: 7 gm	Fat Calories: 63
Total Fat: 7 gm	Dietary Fiber: 3 gm	Sat. Fat: 4 gm	Carbs: 84 gm
Sodium: 270 mg	Fat Component: 19%	Cholesterol: 4 mg	Calcium: 118 mg

Sunrise over Bar Harbor, Maine

French Toast

If left to soak overnight, the crust does not need to be removed.

8 ¾-inch-thick slices
   Italian bread

3 eggs

3 egg whites

1 cup skim milk

1 teaspoon vanilla

pinch of nutmeg

1 tablespoon sugar

1 tablespoon canola oil

Serves 4

Trim crust if bread will soak for less than 2 hours. Place slices in deep-dish pan. Beat together remaining ingredients, except oil. Pour over bread, cover pan and refrigerate, preferably overnight.

Preheat nonstick frying pan over medium-low heat. Lightly brush with butter or canola oil. Fry French Toast on both sides until golden brown.

Serving: 2 slices	Calories: 224	Protein: 11 gm	Fat Calories: 54
Total Fat: 6 gm	Dietary Fiber: 1 gm	Sat. Fat: 1 gm	Carbs: 30 gm
Sodium: 390 mg	Fat Component: 24%	Cholesterol: 108 mg	Calcium: 112 mg

Raspberry Sauce

1½ cups raspberries

1 teaspoon cornstarch

1 tablespoon water

¼ cup maple syrup

¼ cup honey

1 tablespoon lemon juice

Makes 1¾ cups

In a saucepan, mash ¼ cup raspberries. Dissolve cornstarch in water, then whisk into saucepan with remaining ingredients (except whole raspberries). Simmer over medium heat 10 minutes, stirring constantly. Cool 5 minutes before gently folding in whole raspberries.

Serving: 2 tablespoons	Calories: 165	Protein: 0 gm	Fat Calories: 0
Total Fat: 0 gm	Dietary Fiber: 0 gm	Sat. Fat: 0 gm	Carbs: 18 gm
Sodium: 1 mg	Fat Component: 0%	Cholesterol: 0 mg	Calcium: 2 mg

Eggs Benedict Florentine

Perfect for a special weekend brunch.

Serves 4

¾ cup water

1 tablespoon cornstarch

1 tablespoon lemon juice

pinch of salt

pinch of cayenne (optional)

1 teaspoon white pepper

2 egg yolks

1 teaspoon unsalted butter

1 lb. spinach, cooked,
    chopped and drained

1 tablespoon vinegar

8 eggs

4 English muffins

1 teaspoon paprika

Hollandaise Sauce: Boil water in lower pan of double boiler. In the top pan, whisk together ¾ cup water, cornstarch, lemon juice and spices. Stirring constantly, bring to a simmer for 3 minutes. Remove top pan and whisk in egg yolks and butter. Return to heat over boiling water, and stir 3 more minutes. Reduce heat. Press liquid from spinach, then break apart clumps. Mix spinach into sauce. Keep warm.

Eggs: In a large pot, simmer vinegar in 4 inches of water over medium heat. Crack eggs open and carefully drop into boiling water. Cook 3 minutes. Use a slotted spoon to gently remove eggs, and place in a cold water bath. Just before serving, warm eggs for 2 minutes in slowly simmering water.

Putting it all together: Split open and toast English muffins (lightly butter, if desired). Place 2 halves on each plate, spoon sauce over muffin. Use slotted spoon to remove and shake water from eggs, then place in center of muffins. Sprinkle paprika on top.

Serving: 1/4 recipe	Calories: 354	Protein: 22 gm	Fat Calories: 126
Total Fat: 14 gm	Dietary Fiber: 4 gm	Sat. Fat: 5 gm	Carbs: 36 gm
Sodium: 489 mg	Fat Component: 36%	Cholesterol: 460 mg	Calcium: 194 mg

Asparagus and Crab Omelette

Omelettes cook in just 2 minutes!

Serves 4

4 fresh asparagus stalks, cut into ½-inch pieces

¼ cup dry white wine

½ cup fresh crab meat

4 large eggs

4 egg whites

1 tablespoon water

¼ teaspoon salt

½ teaspoon pepper

4 tablespoons grated lowfat Swiss cheese

Lightly steam asparagus in wine. Stir in crab, keeping warm over very low heat.

Preheat 8-inch nonstick omelette pan over medium heat. Whisk eggs, whites, water, salt and pepper in bowl. Brush pan with canola oil. Ladle ½ cup beaten eggs into pan, swirl to distribute. Set on heat for just 1 minute to firm while spreading ¼ of the asparagus, crab and cheese over the omelette.

Hold handle and quickly jerk pan towards you, while tilting far edge over burner. Continue this process and omelette should roll over on itself, or use a spatula to fold in half. Repeat cooking process to make 3 more omelettes.

Serving: 1 omelette	Calories: 142	Protein: 14 gm	Fat Calories: 54
Total Fat: 6 gm	Dietary Fiber: 1 gm	Sat. Fat: 2 gm	Carbs: 4 gm
Sodium: 422 mg	Fat Component: 38%	Cholesterol: 230 mg	Calcium: 116 mg

Juicers can make a great blend of favorite fresh fruits and vegetables for vitamin-rich drinks.

Try mixing apple, cranberry, pear or white grape juice. Add a splash of sparkling water, lemon or lime juice.

Fresh Juice

Combine citrus juices to find the perfect balance of sweet and tart.

Baked Blueberry Porridge

A fruity custard porridge comfort food.

2 eggs

2 tablespoons sugar

½ cup nonfat sour cream

¼ teaspoon vanilla

1 teaspoon baking powder

2 cups cooked grain berries

¼ cup chopped dried
   apples or apricots

¾ cup fresh blueberries

4 pinches each cinnamon,
   sugar and nutmeg

Serves 4

In a large bowl beat eggs with sugar, sour cream, vanilla and baking powder. Stir in cooked grain berries and dried fruit. Gently fold in blueberries.

Spoon into 4 custard cups. Sprinkle with pinches of cinnamon, sugar and nutmeg. Bake at 350º for 25-30 minutes, until center is almost firm. Serve hot.

Serving: 1/4 recipe	Calories: 430	Protein: 11 gm	Fat Calories: 27
Total Fat: 3 gm	Dietary Fiber: 2 gm	Sat. Fat: 1 gm	Carbs: 114 gm
Sodium: 148 mg	Fat Component: 6%	Cholesterol: 39 mg	Calcium: 237 mg

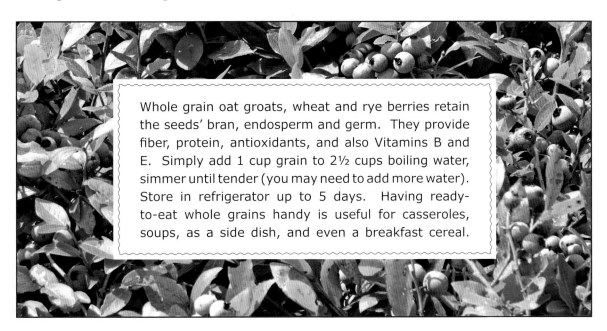

Whole grain oat groats, wheat and rye berries retain the seeds' bran, endosperm and germ. They provide fiber, protein, antioxidants, and also Vitamins B and E. Simply add 1 cup grain to 2½ cups boiling water, simmer until tender (you may need to add more water). Store in refrigerator up to 5 days. Having ready-to-eat whole grains handy is useful for casseroles, soups, as a side dish, and even a breakfast cereal.

Crispy Breakfast Potatoes

Lowfat crispy potatoes to savor.

Serves 4

2 egg whites

1 tablespoon parsley

pinch of salt

1 teaspoon pepper

3 cups shredded potatoes

2 tablespoons grated onion

Beat egg whites and spices in bowl. Add potatoes and onion. Toss to coat.

Heat nonstick frying pan over medium-low heat. Brush with canola oil. Pour ½ of mixture into pan. Cook until crispy on bottom. Use spatula to lift up potatoes, then brush pan with oil and flip. Cook until browned on second side. Keep warm in oven while cooking second batch.

Serving: 1/4 recipe	Calories: 149	Protein: 6 gm	Fat Calories: 0
Total Fat: 0 gm	Dietary Fiber: 3 gm	Sat. Fat: 0 gm	Carbs: 32 gm
Sodium: 71 mg	Fat Component: 0%	Cholesterol: 0 mg	Calcium: 39 mg

Light and easy

Great Granola

Granola is great for breakfast, and on-the-go trail mix.

2 cups quick rolled oats

½ cup wheat germ, bran
    or flakes

½ cup frozen apple juice
    concentrate

1 teaspoon cinnamon

1 tablespoon brown sugar

½ cup raisins and/or
    dried cranberries

Serves 4

Preheat oven to 300º. Mix all ingredients together, except raisins. Spread on cookie sheet. Stirring occasionally, toast in oven 20 minutes, or until light golden brown. Remove from oven and add dried fruit. Cool and store in covered containers or sealable bags to preserve freshness.

Serving: ¾ cup	Calories: 343	Protein: 11 gm	Fat Calories: 36
Total Fat: 4 gm	Dietary Fiber: 7 gm	Sat Fat: 0 gm	Carbs: 67 gm
Sodium: 17 mg	Fat Component: 10%	Cholesterol: 0 mg	Calcium: 48 mg

**Add chopped nuts and dried fruits
for a custom granola crunch.**

Baked Goods

Johnny Cakes...27

Morning Glory Muffins................................28

Zucchini and Everything Nice Muffins...........29

Blueberry Muffins......................................31

Sourdough Rye Rolls.................................32

Buttermilk Fan-Tans...................................33

New London Ship's Biscuits.......................34

Quick Sweet Wheat Bread.........................36

Toasting White Bread................................37

Herbed Buttermilk Bread...........................38

Oatmeal Bread..39

Honeynut Picnic Brown Bread.....................41

Quick Crab Apple Bread............................42

Cinnamon Pecan Bread............................43

Nutritional analyses for breads assume 12 slices per loaf.

Johnny Cakes

Indians taught the early settlers to bake thin corn cakes on flat heated stones. In other areas, they are called hoecakes, ashcakes, mush bread, pone, journey cake or jonakin.

1¼ cups boiling water

1 cup stone-ground
  cornmeal

½ teaspoon salt

½ cup lowfat milk

1 tablespoon canola oil

Makes 24 cakes

In a large saucepan, pour water over cornmeal and salt. Stirring constantly, cook on low heat until water is absorbed. Add milk, stir, then remove from heat.

Heat griddle on medium-low heat, then coat with oil. Drop batter by the tablespoon onto hot griddle and spread into 3-inch rounds. Fry 6 minutes or until golden. Flip to cook on the other side. Serve with maple syrup, honey, or a bowl of homemade soup.

Serving: 3 cakes	Calories: 101	Protein: 3 gm	Fat Calories: 18
Total Fat: 2 gm	Dietary Fiber: 1 gm	Saturated Fat: 0 gm	Carbs: 14 gm
Sodium: 175 mg	Fat Component: 18%	Cholesterol: 1 mg	Calcium: 58 mg

The Jamestown, Rhode Island windmill was built in 1787 to power its millstone for grinding grain and corn. Restored by the Jamestown Historical Society, visitors can take a free self-guided tour to learn about the mechanics of milling corn by wind power. Windmills were an essential part of farming life in the 18th and 19th centuries. Their valuable machinery and high construction cost made it easier to move them rather than build new. The 1812 Sherman Windmill, residing now in Middletown, Rhode Island on the historic site of Prescott Farm, was built in Warren, Rhode Island to serve the distillery trade. From Warren it was moved to Fall River, Massachusetts then to two different sites in Portsmouth, New Hampshire, and was finally acquired by the Newport Restoration Foundation in 1968 and brought back home to Rhode Island.

Morning Glory Muffins

Everything a morning muffin should be.

3 cups shredded bran breakfast cereal

¼ cup canola oil

1 cup golden raisins

1 cup boiling water

2 eggs

2½ cups nonfat buttermilk

¼ cup honey

2¼ cups unbleached flour

1 tablespoon sugar

¼ teaspoon baking soda

1 tablespoon baking powder

Makes 24 muffins

Preheat oven to 375º. Lightly grease muffin cups.

Combine cereal, oil and raisins in mixing bowl. Add boiling water and stir. In a separate bowl, beat eggs, buttermilk and honey. Add liquid to cereal mixture.

In a small bowl, mix flour, sugar, baking soda and powder. Stir into the batter mixture. Cover and let rest 25 minutes. Fill cups ¾ full, bake 25 minutes.

Serving: 1 muffin	Calories: 130	Protein: 4 gm	Fat Calories: 23
Total Fat: 2.5 gm	Dietary Fiber: 3 gm	Saturated Fat: 0 gm	Carbs: 24 gm
Sodium: 189 mg	Fat Component: 17%	Cholesterol: 19 mg	Calcium: 83 mg

Zucchini and Everything Nice Muffins

These moist muffins have fewer than 2 grams of fat each!

1 cup sugar

1 cup shredded zucchini

¾ cup unsweetened
    applesauce

½ cup dried cranberries,
    raisins or chopped dates

2 eggs

2 teaspoons canola oil

2 cups unbleached flour

1 teaspoon baking powder

1 teaspoon baking soda

1 tablespoon cinnamon

pinch of nutmeg or allspice

Makes 12 muffins

Preheat oven to 350º. Lightly grease muffin cups.

In a large bowl, mix sugar, zucchini, applesauce, dried fruit, eggs and oil. In a separate bowl, combine remaining ingredients. Briefly stir flour mixture into liquid ingredients, just until moistened. Divide batter among muffin cups. Bake 20-25 minutes or until toothpick inserted into muffins comes out clean. Remove from tins and cool on wire rack.

Serving: 1 muffin	Calories: 188	Protein: 4 gm	Fat Calories: 18
Total Fat: 2 gm	Dietary Fiber: 2 gm	Saturated Fat: 0.5 gm	Carbs: 40 gm
Sodium: 161 mg	Fat Component: 10%	Cholesterol: 36 mg	Calcium: 34 mg

Maine Wild Blueberries

There are two types of blueberries: lowbush and highbush. Lowbush varieties have smaller fruit that is generally sweeter, with a stronger blueberry flavor. The bigger highbush blueberries have a longer growing season. Both are excellent eaten fresh by the handful, mixed in salads, preserved in jam, baked in pies, muffins, breads, pancakes, and even mashed into BBQ sauce.

Lowbush varieties are commonly called "wild blueberries". They grow in sandy acid soil in New England and northeastern Canada. These rocky "barrens" can support little other growth, but offer conditions favored by these hardy plants. Most wild blueberry fields are still harvested by hand-raking. Commercial sources for these little gems are Maine and the Canadian Maritimes.

Highbush varieties, called "cultivated" blueberries, also thrive in New England, most of the northern U.S., and temperate Canadian regions.

Native Americans used blueberries for many purposes, believing them to have magical powers and healing properties. We now know the blue pigment in blueberry skins is an anthocyanin, a potent antioxidant in the flavonoid group of compounds. Compared to 40 common fruits and vegetables, the USDA rated blueberries number one for their disease-fighting antioxidant capacity.

Blueberry Muffins

This recipe packs in the blueberries.

2 eggs

½ cup nonfat buttermilk

¼ cup melted butter

½ teaspoon vanilla

1 cup sugar

1 tablespoon baking powder

2½ cups unbleached flour

2½ cups fresh blueberries

1 teaspoon cinnamon

1 tablespoon sugar

Makes 12 muffins

Preheat oven to 350º. Grease muffin cups.

In a large bowl, beat eggs, then whip in buttermilk, butter and vanilla. In a separate bowl, mix 1 cup sugar, baking powder and flour. Very briefly stir dry ingredients into liquid; do not blend well.

If blueberries are moist or sticky, toss them with a couple tablespoons of flour to coat. Gently fold blueberries into batter, then spoon into muffin tin. Sprinkle tops with cinnamon and sugar. Bake 25 minutes, or until a toothpick inserted into centers comes out clean.

Serving: 1 muffin	Calories: 208	Protein: 5 gm	Fat Calories: 27
Total Fat: 3 gm	Dietary Fiber: 1 gm	Saturated Fat: 0.5 gm	Carbs: 42 gm
Sodium: 96 mg	Fat Component: 13%	Cholesterol: 37 mg	Calcium: 48 mg

Sourdough Rye Rolls

Sourdough is made in stages over many days.
Use only glass or ceramic bowls, and wooden spoons - no aluminum!

Sourdough Starter:

½ cup rye flour

¼ cup water

1 teaspoon dry yeast

Second Stage Starter:

¾ cup water

1 cup dark or light rye flour

Sponge:

1¾ cups rye flour

1¾ cups unbleached flour

1 teaspoon dry yeast

1 cup water

Final Stage:

1 cup water

2 teaspoons salt

1 tablespoon caraway seed

1¾ cups unbleached flour

Kneading:

2 cups unbleached flour

Optional:

olive oil, seeds, herbs

Makes 24 rolls

Combine sourdough starter ingredients in glass jar. Cover tightly and store 24 hours in a warm location. Mix in second stage ingredients. Cover, and rest 4 hours. This completes the starter. Pour into a ceramic bowl, add sponge ingredients, and cover with a damp cloth to rise in warm place until doubled in bulk. Mix in final stage ingredients, cover, and rest 20 minutes. Turn onto board and work in enough kneading flour to make firm dough. Divide into 24 pieces, shape into round or oblong rolls. If desired, brush with olive oil, press in a bowl of seeds or herbs, and make decorative slashes. Place on baking stone or nonstick sheet. Rise in a warm place until doubled in bulk. Bake 25 minutes at 350º.

Serving: 1 roll	Calories: 151	Protein: 4 gm	Fat Calories: 9
Total Fat: 1 gm	Dietary Fiber: 3 gm	Saturated Fat: 0 gm	Carbs: 32 gm
Sodium: 196 mg	Fat Component: 6%	Cholesterol: 0 mg	Calcium: 10 mg

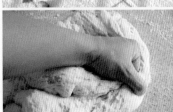

Buttermilk Fan-Tans

A silky dinner roll that will impress your guests.

2 cups nonfat buttermilk

1 package dry yeast
   (2¼ teaspoons)

½ teaspoon baking soda

3 tablespoons sugar

2 tablespoons canola oil

4½ cups unbleached flour

2 tablespoons melted butter

Makes 24 rolls

Heat buttermilk to 110°, then pour into large warmed mixing bowl. Sprinkle yeast over buttermilk, let rest 5 minutes, then stir to dissolve. Mix in baking soda and sugar. Beat well, then stir in oil and 2 cups of flour. Turn out onto floured board and knead in another 2 cups flour. Place dough in a bowl that's been lightly coated with oil; turn to coat all sides. Cover, rise in a warm place until doubled in bulk. Punch down, and knead 2 minutes more. Use remaining ½ cup flour to roll dough into a ¼-inch-thick square, and brush with melted butter. Cut into 1½-inch-wide strips, stack strips five layers high. Cut stacks into 1½-inch-wide sections, and place in nonstick muffin tins with cut edges up. Rise in warm place until doubled in bulk. Bake in 350° oven for 25 minutes.

Serving: 1 roll	Calories: 108	Protein: 4 gm	Fat Calories: 18
Total Fat: 2 gm	Dietary Fiber: 2 gm	Saturated Fat: 0 gm	Carbs: 19 gm
Sodium: 90 mg	Fat Component: 17%	Cholesterol: 1 mg	Calcium: 28 mg

Quick breads (nonyeast baked goods) and yeast breads will both rise better and taste richer with buttermilk. Nonfat buttermilk with live cultures provides probiotic health benefits, a buttery flavor, and no fat! The low acidity in buttermilk tenderizes the flour's gluten, while enhancing the leavening quality of baking soda. Buttermilk can be substituted for milk or water in most recipes, making a slight increase in the quantity to compensate for buttermilk's thicker consistency.

New London Ship's Biscuits

The Thames River gives New London the deepest harbor on the Connecticut coast. Settled in 1646, the city has maintained strong ties to the sea.

2 cups unbleached flour

1 tablespoon baking powder

½ teaspoon baking soda

2 tablespoons canola oil

½ cup nonfat buttermilk

Makes 18 biscuits

Preheat oven to 350º. Grease a cookie sheet.

Mix dry ingredients. Use fingertips to distribute oil through flour. Stir in buttermilk to make a stiff dough. To make dough elastic, pound with a rolling pin to ½-inch thickness. Fold over, and pound thin 8 more times. Roll to ¾-inch thickness, cut into 2-inch rounds. Bake 15 minutes, or until golden.

Serving: 1 biscuit	Calories: 64	Protein: 1 gm	Fat Calories: 18
Total Fat: 2 gm	Dietary Fiber: 0 gm	Saturated Fat: 0 gm	Carbs: 11 gm
Sodium: 65 mg	Fat Component: 28%	Cholesterol: 0 mg	Calcium: 2 mg

Green Mountain
National Forest
Vermont

*Summertime
in
New England
Parks*

White Mountains
State Park
New Hampshire

Cape Cod
National Seashore
Massachusetts

Gillette Castle State Park
East Haddam, Connecticut

North shore of Great Head
Acadia National Park
Bar Harbor, Maine

Local park in Rhode Island

Quick Sweet Wheat Bread

This coarse bread is a good complement to a fruit salad or jam.

Makes 1 loaf

2½ cups whole wheat flour

2 teaspoons baking powder

1 teaspoon baking soda

1 egg

½ cup molasses

¼ cup brown sugar

¼ cup canola oil

1 cup nonfat plain yogurt or buttermilk

Preheat oven to 375º. Grease a 9" x 5" bread pan. Combine flour, baking powder and baking soda. In a separate bowl, beat egg, molasses, brown sugar, oil and yogurt/buttermilk. Briefly stir in flour mixture, just until moistened. Pour into bread pan. Bake 45 minutes, or until loaf sounds hollow when tapped.

Serving: 1 slice	Calories: 177	Protein: 5 gm	Fat Calories: 41
Total Fat: 4.5 gm	Dietary Fiber: 3 gm	Saturated Fat: 1 gm	Carbs: 31 gm
Sodium: 216 mg	Fat Component: 23%	Cholesterol: 18 mg	Calcium: 127 mg

Whole wheat flour is high in fiber, protein, and texture. Whole wheat is distinguished from white flour by the inclusion of the wheat grain's bran and germ. It is milled from hard red spring wheat, but is not as widely favored by many people and bakers as white flour. A new variety, called white whole wheat, has been developed to offer the best of both. White whole wheat contains the protein and fiber of whole grain, but not heavy, bitter dryness of red whole wheat flours. White whole wheat can be substituted for regular white, unbleached white and whole grain flours in recipes.

Toasting White Bread

Softly textured, good homemade bread.

4 teaspoons cornmeal

1 cup warm water

2 tablespoons sugar

1 package dry yeast
   (2¼ teaspoons)

3 cups unbleached flour

¼ teaspoon salt

2 tablespoons butter,
   softened

1 egg white, beaten

Makes 1 loaf

Grease a 9" x 5" bread pan, dust with 2 teaspoons cornmeal. Combine water, sugar and yeast in a small bowl; let rest 10 minutes. In a large bowl, mix flour, salt, butter and the yeast mixture. Turn onto floured board and knead 10 minutes. Lightly coat bowl with oil, place dough in bowl, and turn to coat. Cover bowl, and set in a warm place until doubled in bulk. Punch down and knead 3 minutes, shape, press into pan. Brush with egg white, sprinkle with 2 teaspoons cornmeal. Set in a warm place until doubled in bulk. Bake 40 minutes at 350º, or until loaf sounds hollow when tapped.

Serving: 1 slice	Calories: 148	Protein: 5 gm	Fat Calories: 18
Total Fat: 2 gm	Dietary Fiber: 0 gm	Saturated Fat: 1 gm	Carbs: 29 gm
Sodium: 55 mg	Fat Component: 12%	Cholesterol: 4 mg	Calcium: 7 mg

Herbed Buttermilk Bread

An aromatic and full-flavored loaf.

Makes 2 loaves

2 cups nonfat buttermilk

1 package dry yeast
(2¼ teaspoons)

1 teaspoon baking soda

3 tablespoons sugar

1 tablespoon rosemary

1 tablespoon dill

1 teaspoon garlic powder

¼ cup melted butter

5 cups unbleached flour

2 egg whites, beaten

1 tablespoon sesame seeds,
poppy seeds, or oatmeal

Heat buttermilk to 110º (warm, but not yet hot). Pour into warm large bowl, sprinkle yeast over top, then rest 5 minutes. Stir until yeast dissolves. Mix in baking soda, sugar, herbs, butter and as much flour as you can to yield a workable dough. Turn out onto board to knead in remaining flour.

Coat bowl with oil, place dough in bowl, and turn to coat all sides. Cover, set in warm place to rise until doubled in bulk. Punch down, knead 2 minutes. Divide in half, and shape into loaves. Place in greased bread pans. Brush tops with beaten egg whites, sprinkle and pat in seeds or oatmeal. Rise until doubled in bulk. Bake in 350º oven 45-50 minutes.

Serving: 1 slice	Calories: 118	Protein: 13 gm	Fat Calories: 18
Total Fat: 2 gm	Dietary Fiber: 1 gm	Saturated Fat: 1 gm	Carbs: 24 gm
Sodium: 61 mg	Fat Component: 15%	Cholesterol: 2 mg	Calcium: 35 mg

Oatmeal Bread

An everyday multi-use healthy bread.

2 cups rolled oats

½ teaspoon salt

3 cups boiling water

1 package dry yeast
  (2¼ teaspoons)

¼ cup warm water

½ cup brown sugar

½ cup molasses

¼ cup melted butter

4 cups unbleached flour

1 tablespoon lowfat milk

2 tablespoons quick oats

Makes 2 loaves

In a large bowl, combine rolled oats, salt and boiling water. In a separate bowl, dissolve yeast in warm water, then mix into the oats. Blend in sugar, molasses and butter. Stir in as much flour as you can, then turn onto board to knead in the rest. Knead 10 minutes or until smooth and elastic.

Place dough in bowl coated with oil, and turn to coat all sides. Cover and set in a warm place to rise until doubled in bulk. Punch down, and knead 3 minutes. Shape into two loaves, and place in greased bread pans. Brush top with milk, and sprinkle with quick oats. Cover and let rise until doubled in bulk. Bake in 350º oven 45-50 minutes, or until loaves sound hollow when tapped. Cool on a wire rack.

Serving: 1 slice	Calories: 128	Protein: 4 gm	Fat Calories: 18
Total Fat: 2 gm	Dietary Fiber: 1 gm	Saturated Fat: 1 gm	Carbs: 31 gm
Sodium: 53 mg	Fat Component: 14%	Cholesterol: 0 mg	Calcium: 27 mg

New England Garden and Wildflowers

Top row: Bright Sunset daylilies, Pink Lady Slippers, Siloam Double Classic daylilies
Second row: Camassia, bleeding hearts, Guernsey Cream clematis, Black-eyed Susan
Third Row: Wild flowers and yarrow, What a Peach rose, Moonbeam coreopsis, azaleas
Last row: Annabelle hydrangeas, Francee hosta in shade garden, lupin field

Honeynut Picnic Brown Bread

An easy, fun, quick bread.

1 cup unbleached flour
1 teaspoon baking soda
1 tablespoon baking powder
1 egg
2 cups graham flour
1½ cups nonfat buttermilk
½ cup honey
½ cup dark molasses
¼ cup chopped walnuts

Makes 1 loaf

Preheat oven to 350º. Grease a 9" x 5" loaf pan.

Sift together flour, baking soda and baking powder. Stir in remaining ingredients in the order listed. Pour batter into pan and bake 40 minutes, or until a toothpick inserted into center comes out clean.

Serving: 1 slice	Calories: 152	Protein: 15 gm	Fat Calories: 27
Total Fat: 3 gm	Dietary Fiber: 0 gm	Saturated Fat: 1 gm	Carbs: 31 gm
Sodium: 222 mg	Fat Component: 18%	Cholesterol: 18 mg	Calcium: 103 mg

Quick Crab Apple Bread

Yes, you can use those pretty crab apples!
When they've gone by, use fresh or frozen cranberries.

1 cup chopped crab apples
   or fresh cranberries

½ cup sugar

¼ cup canola oil

1 cup light brown sugar

2 eggs

1 teaspoon lemon juice

2 cups grated apples

3 cups unbleached flour

¼ cup finely chopped nuts

1 teaspoon baking soda

1½ tablespoons baking
   powder

2 teaspoons cinnamon

1 teaspoon nutmeg

¼ teaspoon ground cloves

1 cup nonfat buttermilk

Makes 2 loaves

Preheat oven to 350º. Grease and flour bread pans.

Combine cranberries and sugar. In a large mixing bowl beat oil, brown sugar, eggs and lemon juice, then stir in grated apples. In a third bowl combine flour, nuts, baking soda, baking powder and spices. Alternately, mix dry ingredients and buttermilk into liquid wet mixture. Fold in cranberries, pour batter into bread pans. Bake 1 hour or until toothpick inserted into center comes out clean. Cool breads 10 minutes in pans, then turn out onto wire racks.

Serving: 1 slice	Calories: 156	Protein: 3 gm	Fat Calories: 18
Total Fat: 2 gm	Dietary Fiber: 1 gm	Saturated Fat: 0 gm	Carbs: 29 gm
Sodium: 151 mg	Fat Component: 12%	Cholesterol: 18 mg	Calcium: 61 mg

Male rose-breasted grosbeak in a crab apple

Cinnamon Pecan Bread

Toast and drizzle with honey. Too good to eat alone!

2¼ cups skim milk

2 tablespoons canola oil

½ cup packed brown sugar

½ teaspoon salt

1 package dry yeast
  (2¼ teaspoons)

6½ cups unbleached flour

2 tablespoons skim milk

½ cup sugar

1½ tablespoons cinnamon

½ cup chopped pecans

For tops of loaves:

1 teaspoon sugar

¼ teaspoon cinnamon

Makes 2 loaves

Scald 2¼ cups milk; cool 5 minutes. In a large bowl, combine milk, oil, brown sugar and salt. Sprinkle yeast over top, rest 5 minutes, stir to dissolve. Mix in 5 cups flour, knead in the rest. Work 10 minutes, or until smooth and elastic. Cover and set in a warm place to rise until doubled in bulk. Punch down, knead 3 minutes, then roll out to an 18" square. Brush with milk. Blend cinnamon and sugar together, sprinkle over dough, then pecans. Roll up tightly and slice in half. Place seam sides down in greased and floured bread pans. Pat tops with cinnamon and sugar. Rise in warm place until double in bulk. Bake at 350º for 20 minutes, then tent aluminum foil over loaves, bake 15 minutes more. Cool 10 minutes in pans; then turn out onto wire racks.

Serving: 1 slice	Calories: 176	Protein: 4 gm	Fat Calories: 36
Total Fat: 4 gm	Dietary Fiber: 2 gm	Saturated Fat: 1 gm	Carbs: 36 gm
Sodium: 88 mg	Fat Component: 20%	Cholesterol: 3 mg	Calcium: 33 mg

Appetizers and Finger Food

Lobster Quiche Tarts....................................45

Deviled Shrimp..46

Vegetable Strudel......................................47

Broiled Oysters.......................................49

Smoked Salmon Toasts............................50

Almond Crab Soufflé................................51

Chatham Haddock Balls...........................52

Marvelous Greek Mushrooms.....................54

Garden-Style Antipasto............................55

Crazy Crab Dip.......................................56

Pesto Guacamole.....................................57

Cucumber Finger Tea Sandwiches................59

Apricot Fruit Dip.....................................60

Fourth of July Cherry Bombs.....................61

Appetizers can become a main dish by doubling serving amount per person.

Lobster Quiche Tarts

If there aren't any lobsters in the neighborhood,
you can use 1¼ pounds shrimp or scallops instead.

Tart Shells:

Makes 6 tarts

1½ cups plain nonfat
 bread crumbs

2 tablespoons canola oil

3 tablespoons skim milk

Filling:

3 lobsters, steamed

3 eggs

1 tablespoon vermouth or
 dry white wine

1 cup nonfat sour cream

1 cup grated lowfat
 Swiss Lorraine cheese

Preheat oven to 350º. Lightly grease six nonstick small tart pans (or a 9-inch pie plate). Put crumbs into a mixing bowl, sprinkle with oil and milk. Use a fork to distribute moisture evenly in crumbs. Spoon into prepared pans, pressing to work up the sides and evenly on the bottom. Bake 5 minutes.

Remove meat from lobsters, and cut into bite-size pieces. In a mixing bowl, beat eggs, then whip in wine and sour cream. Stir in lobster and cheese. Spoon into prepared shells. Bake until firm, about 25 minutes. Serve hot, with a big smile.

Serving: 1 tart	Calories: 250	Protein: 31 gm	Fat Calories: 63
Total Fat: 7 gm	Dietary Fiber: 6 gm	Saturated Fat: 1.5 gm	Carbs: 34 gm
Sodium: 192 mg	Fat Component: 25%	Cholesterol: 78 mg	Calcium: 258 mg

Deviled Shrimp

Much more interesting than just plain deviled eggs.

9 large eggs

¼ cup nonfat mayonnaise

½ tablespoon lemon juice

½ teaspoon fresh dill

¼ teaspoon horseradish

¼ teaspoon pepper

½ lb. small bay shrimp

1 tablespoon paprika

Serves 6

Hard-boil eggs (about 7 minutes in boiling water). Plunge into cold water to cool. Peel and slice eggs in half lengthwise. Use a small serrated spoon to gently remove yolks without damaging the whites.

Mash the yolks in a medium mixing bowl, then stir in mayonnaise, lemon juice, dill, horseradish and pepper. Fold in shrimp. Delicately fill egg white halves with mixture, sprinkle with paprika. Arrange on platter, add vegetables or greens for garnish.

Serving: 3 halves	Calories: 64	Protein: 10 gm	Fat Calories: 27
Total Fat: 3 gm	Dietary Fiber: 0 gm	Saturated Fat: 1 gm	Carbs: 3 gm
Sodium: 157 mg	Fat Component: 42%	Cholesterol: 100 mg	Calcium: 20 mg

On nineteenth century New England farms, most egg laying hens roamed free. They did not lay as many eggs as hens do today, because modern hen feed includes egg-inducing vitamins and nutrients. Only the wealthiest New England farms, with a large number of hens, could afford to have a dozen or more eggs at one meal.

Vegetable Strudel

Strudel takes time to make, but the outcome is a delicious delicacy.

Serves 9

2 large onions, chopped

2 cloves garlic, minced

3 stalks celery, chopped

2 tablespoons canola oil

3 carrots, peeled

1 lb. asparagus

2 red peppers

2 cups cooked chopped
  spinach

¼ cup grated Gruyere
  cheese

2 tablespoons chopped
  walnuts

2 tablespoon fresh parsley

½ teaspoon pepper

1 teaspoon of your favorite
  spice

½ cup nonfat bread crumbs

3 cups flour

½ teaspoon baking soda

3 eggs

2 teaspoons vinegar

2½ tablespoons water

1 teaspoon paprika

Sauté onions, garlic and celery in 2 teaspoons oil. Chop carrots, asparagus and peppers, add to pan and cook 5 minutes. Press liquid from spinach. In a large bowl, combine vegetables, cheese, walnuts, spices and bread crumbs. Cover and chill 2 hours.

In a pastry machine, blend flour, baking soda, eggs, vinegar, water and 2 teaspoons oil. On a floured cloth, roll dough very thin. Cut into 9 rectangles of 9" x 12", and gently brush with remaining tablespoon oil. Place 3 sheets of dough in a 9" x 12" baking dish, and cover with half of the filling. Layer 3 more sheets of dough, and cover with remaining filling. Place last 3 sheets on top, then dust with paprika. Use a sharp knife to mark cutting lines through top pastry layer. Bake at 350º for 30 minutes, or until golden.

Serving: 1/9 recipe	Calories: 204	Protein: 8 gm	Fat Calories: 63
Total Fat: 7 gm	Dietary Fiber: 4 gm	Saturated Fat: 1 gm	Carbs: 28 gm
Sodium: 120 mg	Fat Component: 31%	Cholesterol: 38 mg	Calcium: 112 mg

Somesville, Maine
Mount Desert Island

Clams

Steamers are soft-shell clams found north of Cape Cod, and are always cooked. The most common clams for chowder and batter-dipping are hard-shell quahogs and littlenecks. Scrub, soak 1 hour in cold water mixed with ¼-cup flour, rinse well. Discard any open clams. Steam and shuck, discarding the black "beard".

Mussels

Blue mussels are dredged or dug from New England's shallow muddy bays, tidal ponds and salty river beds.   Discard any with broken shells. Scrub, soak 1 hour in cold water mixed with ¼-cup flour, rinse well. Steam and shuck, discarding the black filament, and any mussels that are still closed after steaming.

Oysters

Northern oysters are best in months with an 'R' (not when spawning May-August). Scrub well, discard if broken or not closed when handled. Pry open with an oyster knife. To open easily: bake 4 minutes at 400º, plunge into ice water, drain. Scrape out meat, check for shell fragments.   Strain oyster liqueur through fine muslin.

Broiled Oysters

If you appreciate oysters, this is your recipe!

2 dozen fresh oysters

3 egg whites

2 tablespoons parsley

½ teaspoon white pepper

¼ teaspoon garlic powder

1 cup nonfat bread crumbs

1½ cups grated lowfat
    Swiss Lorraine cheese

Serves 4

See facing page for instructions to clean and open oysters. Place open oysters in a shallow pan.

In a small bowl, beat egg whites and spices until foamy. Spread about 1 teaspoon of the mixture on each oyster, then sprinkle with 2 teaspoons bread-crumbs and 1 tablespoon grated cheese. Place on middle rack under preheated broiler; watch carefully. When the cheese is golden, they're done.

Serving: 6 oysters	Calories: 351	Protein: 16 gm	Fat Calories: 72
Total Fat: 8 gm	Dietary Fiber: 2 gm	Saturated Fat: 3 gm	Carbs: 28 gm
Sodium: 320 mg	Fat Component: 21%	Cholesterol: 103 mg	Calcium: 120 mg

Smoked Salmon Toasts

Either hot smoked (dry) or cold smoked (moist) salmon can be used.

2 tablespoons sesame
   seeds

1 scallion, finely chopped

½ lb. smoked salmon

1 tablespoon vermouth

2 egg whites, beaten

½ teaspoon minced garlic

½ teaspoon cornstarch

6 slices light wheat or
   oatmeal bread

2 teaspoons canola oil

Serves 6

In a nonstick frying pan over medium heat, briefly toast sesame seeds until light brown. Add scallion and stir until wilted. Transfer to a mixing bowl. Cut smoked salmon into small pieces and add to mixing bowl. Stir in vermouth, beaten egg whites, garlic and cornstarch. Let rest 15 minutes.

Trim crust from bread, cut each into 4 triangles, and spread with 1 tablespoon salmon mixture. Coat frying pan with 1 teaspoon oil, and warm on medium-high heat. Place pieces salmon-side down in pan, and fry until golden brown. Flip pieces to briefly toast the bread. Keep warm in 300º oven. Repeat frying for second batch. Serve hot.

Serving: 4 pieces	Calories: 143	Protein: 10 gm	Fat Calories: 45
Total Fat: 5 gm	Dietary Fiber: 1 gm	Saturated Fat: 1 gm	Carbs: 14 gm
Sodium: 320 mg	Fat Component: 31%	Cholesterol: 6 mg	Calcium: 54 mg

New Hampshire and Maine share Gosport Harbor and its Isles of Shoals, where enormous schools of salmon greeted European settlers. Some of the early arrivals came just to set up fishing camps on the Isles. In the 1890s Celia Thaxter, daughter of a lighthouse keeper on Appledore Island, wrote *An Island Garden*. Her magnificent garden has been restored, and summer boat tours can be booked at "Visiting Celia Thaxter's Garden" on: www.sml.cornell.edu

Almond Crab Soufflé

This soufflé really displays the quality of fresh crab.

18 oz. fresh crab meat

3 eggs, separated

½ cup skim milk

¼ cup nonfat powdered milk

1 small onion, finely diced

1 tablespoon canola oil

3 tablespoons flour

salt to taste

½ teaspoon white pepper

3 tablespoons brandy

¼ teaspoon saffron

3 tablespoons almond slivers, chopped

Serves 6

Preheat oven to 325º and set a kettle of water to boil. Check crab meat for shells.

In a small metal bowl, beat egg whites until firm. In a large bowl, beat yolks, then beat in milks.

Sauté onion in oil over medium heat until clear. Add crab meat, cook 1 minute. Stir in flour, salt and pepper, cook 3 minutes more. Add brandy, saffron and almonds, cook another minute, then mix into beaten yolk mixture. Gently fold in egg whites.

Grease a small ceramic dish. Spoon mixture into dish, then set into a large deep baking dish. Pour boiling water into the large baking dish to half the height of soufflé dish. Bake 50 minutes. Serve hot or cold – with fruit, rice crackers, and a good wine.

Serving: 1/6 recipe	Calories: 174	Protein: 18 gm	Fat Calories: 54
Total Fat: 6 gm	Dietary Fiber: 1 gm	Saturated Fat: 2 gm	Carbs: 8 gm
Sodium: 458 mg	Fat Component: 31%	Cholesterol: 152 mg	Calcium: 114 mg

Chatham Haddock Balls

Spice these up any way you like!

Serves 8

1½ lbs. haddock or any
    firm white fish

6 medium potatoes, baked

2 eggs

3 tablespoons skim milk

2 tablespoons grated onion

2 tablespoons grated
    Parmesan cheese

1 tablespoon lemon juice

salt and pepper to taste

2 tablespoons canola oil

½ cup skim milk

¼ cup bread crumbs

Steam haddock 20 minutes, or until cooked through. Cool, drain, and pat dry. Process haddock through meat grinder or chop into very small pieces. Rice or mash potatoes (discard skins), and mix with fish. Beat in eggs, 3 tablespoons milk, onion, cheese, lemon juice and seasoning. Roll into 1-inch balls.

Warm oil in a nonstick frying pan on medium-high heat. Pour ½ cup milk into a small bowl. Dip haddock balls in milk, then roll in bread crumbs. Fry, swirling frequently to prevent sticking, until golden brown. Serve hot with seafood or tartare sauce.

Serving: 1/8 recipe	Calories: 194	Protein: 17 gm	Fat Calories: 54
Total Fat: 6 gm	Dietary Fiber: 1 gm	Saturated Fat: 1 gm	Carbs: 14 gm
Sodium: 100 mg	Fat Component: 28%	Cholesterol: 83 mg	Calcium: 68 mg

For 400 years, the history of Cape Cod has been tied to the groundfishing industry. Haddock, cod, redfish and flounder are the natural species of New England's groundfish stocks. Undersea ecology is now continuously studied, and beginning to be understood. New fishing practices have helped to restore groundfish habitat. In offshore banks of up to 600 feet deep, the haddock population has rebounded.

Chatham, Massachusetts

Atlantic Gray Seals

Adult males are 8' long, and females 6'. Gray seals inhabit the inshore waters of Maine and Massachusetts. They dive up to 475' to feed on fish and invertebrates.

Harbor Seals

The most common local seal. About five feet long, plump, varying in color and spots. Their curious faces pop up alongside boats – but they are shy.

Marine Mammal Summer Residents

Humpback Whales

Huge quantities of plankton draw humpbacks to their New England feeding area from April-November. They blow water spouts 20' high in the air, which helps the whale watchers find them.

Humpbacks display a unique tail fin pattern when starting a dive. Researchers catalog the tail images to identify individuals and also track migration patterns.

Saddle-backed Dolphin

Also called the Common dolphin, they reside in these waters June-October. The playful 7' dolphins are often seen riding a boat's bow wave. New England's other summer dolphins are the Bottle-Nosed Dolphin, Harbor Porpoise, Atlantic White-sided Dolphin, and White-beaked Dolphin. The bounty of small fish on the surface provides attractive dolphin food.

Marvelous Greek Mushrooms

These are always a hit with company, with warm garlic toast on the side.

1 lb. fresh mushrooms

2 cups vegetable broth
   (from bouillon cubes)

2 tablespoons lemon juice

1 tablespoon virgin olive oil

Tied cheesecloth containing:

12 peppercorns

4" stalk of celery

4 sprigs parsley

2 cloves garlic

sprig of fresh thyme,
   or 2 pinches dried thyme

6 coriander seeds

Serves 4

Wash mushrooms and trim dried ends of stems. If mushrooms are large, cut into quarters; if medium-sized, cut in half.

In a large pot, boil broth, lemon juice, olive oil and spice bag. Add mushrooms and stir. Cover pot, reduce heat and simmer 10 minutes. Remove mushrooms with a slotted spoon, and arrange in a serving dish. Rapidly boil down liquid until it is reduced to about ½ cup. Remove spice bag and adjust seasonings. Pour sauce over mushrooms. Serve hot or cold.

Serving: 1/4 recipe	Calories: 66	Protein: 5 gm	Fat Calories: 23
Total Fat: 2.5 gm	Dietary Fiber: 0 gm	Saturated Fat: 0 gm	Carbs: 11 gm
Sodium: 58 mg	Fat Component: 34%	Cholesterol: 0 mg	Calcium: 55 mg

Garden-Style Antipasto

For the best flavor, use fresh-cut herbs.

Serves 4

4 large fresh tomatoes

2 peppers, different colors

1 cup julienne carrots

2 celery stalks, sliced
    into thin strips

2 oz. part-skim
    mozzarella cheese

8 pitted Italian olives

1 tablespoon olive oil

1 tablespoon lime juice

1 tablespoon wine vinegar

3 tablespoons white wine

1 clove garlic, crushed

1 tablespoon summer
    savory

¼ cup chopped parsley

1 tablespoon basil

salt and pepper to taste

Slice tomatoes into thick rounds on individual serving plates. Slice peppers into strips. Cut cheese into wedges. Place vegetables and olives in the middle of each plate.

Combine remaining ingredients in a jar. Shake for at least 3 minutes. Sprinkle over vegetables and mozzarella. Chill antipasto plates before serving.

Serving: 1/4 recipe	Calories: 161	Protein: 6 gm	Fat Calories: 72
Total Fat: 8 gm	Dietary Fiber: 5 gm	Saturated Fat: 2.5 gm	Carbs: 17 gm
Sodium: 278 mg	Fat Component: 45%	Cholesterol: 10 mg	Calcium: 157 mg

Antipasto is about welcoming the meal to the table with a fresh start. An antipasto features assorted raw and lightly steamed peak-season vegetables. Use it to present unique local cheeses and exotic imports. This is how to show off your garden's bounty or shopping skills at the farmers' market!

Crazy Crab Dip

Serve this zesty dip hot or cold, with toast points or crackers for dipping.

16 oz. fresh crab meat

1 cup nonfat sour cream

8 oz. nonfat cream cheese,
    at room temperature

2 teaspoons finely
    chopped scallion

1 teaspoon lemon juice

1 tablespoon dry sherry

dash of hot pepper sauce

salt and pepper to taste

½ cup chopped water
    chestnuts

½ cup grated lowfat
    white Cheddar

Serves 6

Preheat oven to 350º. Carefully check crab meat for shell pieces. Use electric beaters to whip sour cream, cream cheese, scallion, lemon juice, sherry, hot pepper sauce, salt and pepper. Stir in chopped water chestnuts and crab meat. Spoon into 6 small baking cups, sprinkle with Cheddar, and bake 25 minutes.

Serving: 1/6 recipe	Calories: 130	Protein: 21 gm	Fat Calories: 18
Total Fat: 2 gm	Dietary Fiber: 0 gm	Saturated Fat: 0.5 gm	Carbs: 10 gm
Sodium: 379 mg	Fat Component: 14%	Cholesterol: 59 mg	Calcium: 120 mg

Pesto Guacamole

The pesto blend adds a nice zing to guacamole.

1 cup nonfat plain yogurt
  and/or sour cream

2 cloves garlic, crushed

¾ cup packed basil leaves

½ tablespoon olive oil

1 tablespoon grated onion

4-8 drops hot pepper sauce

1 tablespoon Parmesan

1 tablespoon pine nuts

2 medium-size avocados

2 teaspoons lemon or lime
  juice

3 tablespoons pimiento

salt and pepper to taste

Serves 4

In a blender, whip yogurt / sour cream. With blender running, drop in garlic, basil leaves, olive oil, onion, hot pepper sauce, Parmesan cheese and pine nuts. Blend until smooth. In a mixing bowl, mash avocado and sprinkle with juice.   Fold blender mixture into avocado, stir in pimiento, salt and pepper.

Serving: 1/4 cup	Calories: 66	Protein: 2 gm	Fat Calories: 36
Total Fat: 4 gm	Dietary Fiber: 3 gm	Saturated Fat: 1 gm	Carbs: 6 gm
Sodium: 51 mg	Fat Component: 55%	Cholesterol: 1 mg	Calcium: 30 mg

Cocktails

As the sun sinks below the yardarm...

Red Rickey
2 oz. vodka
½ oz. Creme de Cassis
2 teaspoons lime juice
1 oz. soda water

Pour over ice, stir, strain.

Sangria Pitcher Party
Serves 6

juice of 3 lemons
¾ cup brandy
½ cup orange liqueur
½ cup sugar
4 cups red wine
¾ cup pitted cherry halves
thinly sliced fruit:
orange, lemon, 2 peaches

Combine everything
in a larger pitcher.
Stir and chill well.
Distribute fruit in glasses.
Stir again, pour over fruit.

Recipes make 1 drink
(except Sangria)
1 shot = 1 oz.

Strawberry Daiquiri
2 oz. rum
6 hulled strawberries
1 teaspoon lime juice
1 tablespoon sugar
1 cup shaved ice

Process in blender.

Party Margaritas
2 oz. tequila
½ oz. triple sec
1 T. powdered sugar
2 tsp. lime or cherry juice
½ cup crushed ice

Wet glass rim, dip in salt.
Shake ingredients, pour.

Martini Classic
3 oz. gin
1 oz. vermouth

Pour over ice.
Shake or stir.
Strain into glass.
Add stuffed olive.

Cucumber Finger Tea Sandwiches

Tantalizing little finger hors d'oeuvres.

¼ cup nonfat mayonnaise

½ teaspoon lemon juice

pinch of dill

pinch of garlic powder

pinch of salt

3 pinches of pepper

1 large cucumber, chilled

8 slices sourdough bread

1 teaspoon paprika

2 tablespoons chives

Serves 4

Combine mayonnaise, lemon juice, dill, garlic, salt and pepper in small mixing bowl. Adjust seasonings to taste. Peel cucumber and slice into rounds.

Use a 2-inch round cookie cutter, or small glass, to cut rounds from bread (exclude crust). Spread mayonnaise mix on the bread rounds, and place a slice of cucumber on top. Double stack, then sprinkle with paprika and chives.

Serving: 1 sandwich	Calories: 180	Protein: 5 gm	Fat Calories: 18
Total Fat: 2 gm	Dietary Fiber: 2 gm	Saturated Fat: 0.5 gm	Carbs: 33 gm
Sodium: 519 mg	Fat Component: 10%	Cholesterol: 0 mg	Calcium: 48 mg

Apricot Fruit Dip

This dip is wonderful for slices of any firm fruit.

2 cups dried apricots

4 cups orange juice

½ cup unsweetened applesauce

¼ cup honey

½ teaspoon cinnamon

¼ teaspoon nutmeg

1 teaspoon vanilla

Makes 3 cups

Chop dried apricots into small pieces. Place in a non-aluminum saucepan with orange juice over medium heat. Use a wooden spoon to mash apricots as the mixture is brought to a boil. Reduce heat and simmer until liquid is absorbed. Remove from stove. Mix in remaining ingredients, cover and chill.

Serving: 1/4 cup	Calories: 118	Protein: 1 gm	Fat Calories: 0
Total Fat: 0 gm	Dietary Fiber: 2 gm	Saturated Fat: 0 gm	Carbs: 30 gm
Sodium: 4 mg	Fat Component: 0%	Cholesterol: 0 mg	Calcium: 19 mg

Apricot cultivars such as Goldbar, Goldstrike, Tilton and Wenatchee can be grown as far north as zone 4, which is just about anywhere in New England.

Fourth of July Cherry Bombs

A burst-in-your-mouth cherry tomato treat.

1 pint cherry tomatoes

16 oz. nonfat cream
cheese, softened

1 teaspoon grated onion

1 tablespoon fresh cilantro

½ teaspoon cumin

pinch of cayenne

salt and pepper to taste

1 cup cooked shrimp

1 teaspoon paprika

Serves 6

Cut tops off cherry tomatoes. With a small serrated teaspoon, scoop out pulp and put it into a small mixing bowl. Add cream cheese, onion and spices (except paprika). Use a fork to blend well.

Drain, dry and chop shrimp into small pieces, then fold into mixture. Squeeze through a pastry bag to fill cherry tomatoes. Sprinkle with paprika.

Serving: 1/6 recipe	Calories: 57	Protein: 8 gm	Fat Calories: 5
Total Fat: 0.5 gm	Dietary Fiber: 1 gm	Saturated Fat: 0 gm	Carbs: 4 gm
Sodium: 160 mg	Fat Component: 8%	Cholesterol: 49 mg	Calcium: 30 mg

Fireworks celebrations in Concord, Massachusetts,
Providence, Rhode Island and Hartford, Connecticut.

Fresh Greens and Salads

Apple-Raisin Cole Slaw.............................63

Marinated Lentil and Leek Salad...................64

Egg and Potato Salad..............................65

Rainbow Pepper Pasta Salad........................67

Maine Shrimp Salad................................68

Creamy Beets......................................69

Seared Tuna with Endive...........................70

Spinach and Pine Nut Salad........................71

Robust Romaine and Tomato Basil Vinaigrette.72

Peachy-Keen Mint Mold.............................74

Honey-French Dressing.............................75

Smooth Yogurt-Dill Dressing.......................75

Salads can become a complete lunch by doubling the serving per person.

Apple-Raisin Cole Slaw

This cole slaw is unlike any other, and wicked good!

1 cup nonfat plain yogurt

¼ cup nonfat mayonnaise

2 tablespoons honey

pinch of salt

¼ teaspoon white pepper

1 tablespoon lemon juice

3 grated McIntosh or
   Granny Smith apples

1 cup golden raisins

4 cups finely grated cabbage

1½ cups grated carrots

Serves 8

Process yogurt, mayonnaise, honey, salt and pepper in a blender. In a large bowl, sprinkle lemon juice over apples, then mix in raisins, cabbage, carrots and dressing. Cover and chill well before serving.

Serving: 1/8 recipe	Calories: 124	Protein: 4 gm	Fat Calories: 5
Total Fat: 0.5 gm	Dietary Fiber: 12 gm	Saturated Fat: 0 gm	Carbs: 38 gm
Sodium: 124 mg	Fat Component: 4%	Cholesterol: 1 mg	Calcium: 65 mg

Marinated Lentil and Leek Salad

Colored lentils can be used interchangeably with minimal flavor variation.

3 cups water

1 cup dried lentils

10"-12" of white leek stalks

¼ teaspoon ground cloves

2 bay leaves

1 clove garlic, minced

1 teaspoon oregano

1 tablespoon olive oil

2 tablespoons wine vinegar

1 cup chopped, peeled and
    drained tomatoes

2 tablespoons finely
    chopped chives

salt and pepper to taste

Serves 6

Pour water into pot to boil. Rinse lentils. Remove green leaves and root tip from leeks. Thoroughly rinse out the leek's tender white stalks, and chop into ¼-inch rounds. Add lentils, chopped leeks, cloves, bay leaves and garlic to boiling water. When lentils are tender, about 45 minutes, drain. Discard bay leaves. Mix in remaining ingredients. Chill well.

Serving: 1/6 recipe	Calories: 161	Protein: 9 gm	Fat Calories: 27
Total Fat: 3 gm	Dietary Fiber: 10 gm	Saturated Fat: 1 gm	Carbs: 20 gm
Sodium: 100 mg	Fat Component: 17%	Cholesterol: 0 mg	Calcium: 32 mg

Egg and Potato Salad

A simple summer classic.

3 lbs. red potatoes (about 9 medium-size spuds)

4 eggs

2 tablespoons canola oil

1 tablespoon lemon juice

½ small onion, grated

1 teaspoon dill

½ teaspoon garlic powder

½ cup finely chopped celery

½ cup nonfat mayonnaise

¼ cup nonfat buttermilk or sour cream

½ teaspoon salt

1 teaspoon pepper

Serves 8

Wash and peel potatoes. Dice into bite-size pieces and boil in water. Add eggs to pot and hard-boil (about 6 minutes). Use a slotted spoon to remove eggs, set in cold water, then shell. Chop eggs and chill. When potatoes are tender, drain and chill with eggs.

In a small mixing bowl, combine remaining ingredients for dressing. When everything is cold, fold dressing into potatoes. Cover and chill. Garnish with chives.

Serving: 1/8 recipe	Calories: 215	Protein: 8 gm	Fat Calories: 36
Total Fat: 4 gm	Dietary Fiber: 4 gm	Saturated Fat: 1 gm	Carbs: 32 gm
Sodium: 300 mg	Fat Component: 17%	Cholesterol: 108 mg	Calcium: 59 mg

Smooth kayaking on Lake Champlain, VT

Gerrish Island, ME sunrise

Biking along Narragansett Bay, RI

Annual Queechee Balloon Festival, VT

A gorgeous day in CT for strolling along the shore

Waterfalls in the Green Mountains, VT

Scenic railroad Crawford Notch, NH

Antique airplane show rendezvous, ME

The Clay Cliffs, Aquinna Martha's Vineyard, MA

Sailing Frenchman Bay Bar Harbor, ME

Harbor sunset, CT

Canoes at the ready Scarborough Marsh, ME

Exploring New England

New England has fun activities available for all ages and interests. Acadia National Park's free programs on flora, fauna and the natural history of Mount Desert Island provide captivating outings. New England hosts numerous summer parades, music, arts and crafts fairs. Historic museums and reenactment settlements depict a simpler, but maybe not easier, time. For most, exploring includes time and space to play – driving, strolling, hiking, biking, swimming, paddling, sailing, golfing or flying through the area's exquisite coast, mountains, woods and city landscapes.

Rainbow Pepper Pasta Salad

Garnish with greens, olives, cheese and corn.

Serves 6

1 lb. dry multicolored bow-tie or spiral pasta

1 medium-sized onion

4 bell peppers in assorted colors (red, yellow, purple, orange, green)

2 tablespoons canola oil

¼ cup chopped sundried tomatoes

¼ cup herbed vinegar

1 clove garlic, minced

½ teaspoon oregano

½ teaspoon basil

½ teaspoon dill

¼ cup diced pimientos

½ cup nonfat mayonnaise

2 teaspoons lemon juice

salt and pepper to taste

Boil pasta just until tender; drain. Transfer to a large bowl, cover and chill.

Cut onion and peppers into thin slices. Heat oil in a large skillet Lightly stir-fry onion and peppers, just until onions are clear. Mix in sundried tomatoes. Add vegetables to pasta, cover and chill.

Combine remaining ingredients to make dressing. Pour over pasta, toss gently and chill until served.

Serving: 2 tablespoons	Calories: 78	Protein: 0 gm	Fat Calories: 45
Total Fat: 5 gm	Dietary Fiber: 0 gm	Saturated Fat: 1 gm	Carbs: 5 gm
Sodium: 16 mg	Fat Component: 58%	Cholesterol: 0 mg	Calcium: 5 mg

Peppers and  Pasta

Maine Shrimp Salad

Pat shrimp dry in a kitchen towel, or salad will be watery.

1 cup nonfat cottage cheese

1 teaspoon lemon juice

1½ tablespoons fresh dill

¼ teaspoon garlic powder

¼ teaspoon onion powder

½ teaspoon pepper

1 lb. small cooked shrimp, peeled and deveined

¾ cup peeled, seeded and finely diced cucumber

Serves 6

Process all ingredients, except shrimp and cucumber, in a blender until smooth. Pour mixture over shrimp and cucumber. Cover and chill at least 2 hours.

Serving: 1/5 recipe	Calories: 125	Protein: 23 gm	Fat Calories: 18
Total Fat: 2 gm	Dietary Fiber: 0 gm	Saturated Fat: 1 gm	Carbs: 4 gm
Sodium: 205 mg	Fat Component: 14%	Cholesterol: 180 mg	Calcium: 97 mg

Northern shrimp and fishing vessels at Portland, Maine.

The Gulf of Maine fishery for northern shrimp is cooperatively managed and harvested by New Hampshire, Maine and Massachusetts. Boats can haul in over 1,000 pounds of shrimp per trip. Averaging about 1 inch in length, the small northern shrimp are tender and sweet.

Creamy Beets

Similar to borscht (beet soup), but without the liquid.

6 medium-sized beets

¾ cup nonfat sour cream

1 tablespoon cider vinegar

1 tablespoon grated onion

1 tablespoon parsley

salt and pepper to taste

Serves 4

Scrub beets. Simmer in water until tender, about 40 minutes. Drain, cool, peel and slice into rounds.

In a small bowl, combine all remaining ingredients. Mix beets with sauce. Chill well before serving.

Serving: 1/4 recipe	Calories: 55	Protein: 3 gm	Fat Calories: 0
Total Fat: 0 gm	Dietary Fiber: 1 gm	Saturated Fat: 0 gm	Carbs: 11 gm
Sodium: 117 mg	Fat Component: 0%	Cholesterol: 1 mg	Calcium: 84 mg

Seared Tuna with Endive

Top with fresh fine herbs, like rosemary and sage.

2 tablespoons olive oil

1 clove garlic, halved

2 tablespoons frozen orange juice concentrate

1 tablespoon wine vinegar

¼ cup concentrated vegetable broth

1 lb. thick tuna steak

1 tablespoon pepper

1 tablespoon canola oil

2 cups chicory (curly endive)

1 head Boston bibb lettuce

2 Belgian endives

24 baby pickled beets

12 cherry or 2 heirloom tomatoes

½ cucumber

Serves 4

Combine olive oil, garlic, juice concentrate, vinegar, and broth in a jar. Chill well, then discard garlic.

Slice tuna into 2-inch-wide strips. Rub with ground pepper. Heat canola oil in a nonstick pan. Sear tuna on all four sides, to medium-rare or as desired. Slice strips into ¼-inch-wide cubes. Chill.

When everything is cold, wash, dry and arrange greens on salad plates. Cut tomatoes to show shape. Peel cucumber, slice into thin strips. Place vegetables and tuna on salads. Shake dressing, pour 2 tablespoons onto each serving. Garnish.

Serving: 1/4 recipe	Calories: 160	Protein: 5 gm	Fat Calories: 63
Total Fat: 7 gm	Dietary Fiber: 8 gm	Saturated Fat: 2 gm	Carbs: 11 gm
Sodium: 200 mg	Fat Component: 39%	Cholesterol: 4 mg	Calcium: 226 mg

Spinach and Pine Nut Salad

Select the smallest spinach leaves; they will be the tenderest.

1 lb. fresh baby spinach

½ purple onion

1 orange

1 clove garlic

2 tablespoons nonfat
   buttermilk or sour cream

1 tablespoon olive oil

1 tablespoon balsamic
   vinegar

1 teaspoon lemon juice

salt and pepper to taste

2 tablespoons pine nuts

Serves 4

Rinse and dry spinach. Thinly slice onion. Separate sections from orange, discarding pith. Halve garlic, rub on the inside of salad bowl, then mince and put into blender. Combine spinach, onion and orange wedges in bowl; chill. Add all remaining ingredients to blender, except pine nuts, and process until smooth. Chill dressing. Just before serving, toss salad with dressing. Divide onto plates, and sprinkle with nuts.

Serving: 1/4 recipe	Calories: 87	Protein: 4 gm	Fat Calories: 54
Total Fat: 6 gm	Dietary Fiber: 1 gm	Saturated Fat: 1 gm	Carbs: 5 gm
Sodium: 66 mg	Fat Component: 62%	Cholesterol: 0 mg	Calcium: 19 mg

Robust Romaine and Tomato Basil Vinaigrette

Dressing:

Serves 6

3 large very ripe tomatoes

1 large clove minced garlic

1 tablespoon olive oil

¼ cup finely chopped basil

¼ teaspoon dry mustard

1 teaspoon sugar

½ teaspoon salt

1 teaspoon paprika

3 tablespoons dried minced onion

2 tablespoons parsley

¼ cup balsamic vinegar

Salad:

2 heads romaine lettuce

28 nasturtium flowers

½ cup peeled grated carrot

2 tablespoons fresh basil, parsley and/or dill

This dressing enhances any fresh vegetable salad – like the sliced tomato, buffalo mozzarella and basil platter on the front cover.

Chop tomatoes and press through a fine sieve into mixing bowl. Discard seeds and skin. Drain off excess liquid, leaving about 1 cup tomato mash.

Lightly sauté garlic in olive oil over medium heat until tender. Add basil and dry mustard, cook 1 minute more. Remove from heat, whisk in sugar and salt until dissolved. Pour into tomato mash, then whisk in remaining dressing ingredients. Chill at least 12 hours, then shake well, and adjust spices to taste.

Wash, dry and tear romaine. Combine in salad bowl with nasturtiums, grated carrot and herbs. Toss with dressing, chill until served.

Serving: 1/6 recipe	Calories: 78	Protein: 2 gm	Fat Calories: 36
Total Fat: 4 gm	Dietary Fiber: 6 gm	Saturated Fat: 1 gm	Carbs: 10 gm
Sodium: 90 mg	Fat Component: 46%	Cholesterol: 0 mg	Calcium: 95 mg

Tomatoes

The four tomato types are beefsteak, plum, globe and cherry/grape. Within these are hundreds of cultivars, heirlooms and exotic varieties. While red is ordinary, some ripen yellow, orange, pink, purple or striped.

Tomatoes are an excellent source of vitamins that protect against certain cancers. Happy to grow in any sunny spot, even patio containers will do.

To make tomato sauce: poach, peel and dice very ripe tomatoes. Simmer down to desired thickness. Add sautéed vegetables and spices. Freeze in small batches. Homemade sauce is at its best in midwinter!

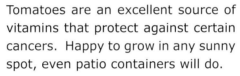

Peachy-Keen Mint Mold

Gelatins can also be made in individual serving molds.

Serves 6

2 tablespoons gelatin
  (3 small packets)

½ cup cold water

1½ cups peeled and sliced
  peaches

2 cups boiling water

¼ cup mint leaves

4 drops green food coloring

¾ cup sugar

pinch of salt

2 teaspoons lemon juice

In a large bowl, soak gelatin in cold water. Poach peaches 5 minutes in boiling water. Remove from heat, and use a slotted spoon to remove peaches. Steep mint leaves in hot peach juice 10 minutes, then strain into gelatin mixture. Stir in color, sugar, salt and lemon juice, mixing until completely dissolved.

Rinse, but don't dry mold. Pour mixture ½-inch deep in mold. Arrange peaches, chill until firm. Pour in half of the remaining mixture; evenly distribute remaining peaches, chill. When set, pour in remaining mixture. (If needed, briefly warm mixture to liquidized.)

To unmold, lower bottom of mold into hot water. Dry off, then turn onto serving platter.

Serving: 1/6 recipe	Calories: 96	Protein: 3 gm	Fat Calories: 0
Total Fat: 0 gm	Dietary Fiber: 1 gm	Saturated Fat: 0 gm	Carbs: 22 gm
Sodium: 26 mg	Fat Component: 0%	Cholesterol: 0 mg	Calcium: 10 mg

Honey-French Dressing

This fabulous dressing is a stock item in our fridge.

¼ cup low-sodium ketchup

2 tablespoons olive oil

2 tablespoons canola oil

2 tablespoons lemon juice

2 tablespoons wine vinegar

¼ cup honey

salt, pepper and Tabasco
     sauce to taste

Makes 1¼ cups

With all ingredients at room temperature, combine in a glass jar with tight-fitting lid. Shake well to blend. Chill. Shake well before pouring.

Serving: 2 tablespoons	Calories: 83	Protein: 0 gm	Fat Calories: 36
Total Fat: 4 gm	Dietary Fiber: 0 gm	Saturated Fat: 1 gm	Carbs: 13 gm
Sodium: 69 mg	Fat Component: 43%	Cholesterol: 0 mg	Calcium: 1 mg

Smooth Yogurt-Dill Dressing

½ cup nonfat mayonnaise

¾ cup nonfat plain yogurt

1 clove garlic, pressed

1 tablespoon fresh dill

1 teaspoon chervil

1 teaspoon parsley

salt and pepper to taste

Makes 1¼ cups

Whisk together all ingredients. Chill well.

Serving: 2 tablespoons	Calories: 18	Protein: 1 gm	Fat Calories: 0
Total Fat: 0 gm	Dietary Fiber: 0 gm	Saturated Fat: 0 gm	Carbs: 3 gm
Sodium: 52 mg	Fat Component: 0%	Cholesterol: 0 mg	Calcium: 33 mg

Soups, Stews and Chowders

Creamy Cold Cucumber Soup......................77

Curried Carrot Soup......................78

Zesty Lentil Stew......................79

Vegetable Soup with Dumplings..................81

Hearty Vegetable Minestrone......................82

Cream of Asparagus......................83

Northend Lobster Bouillabaisse..................84

Quick Gazpacho......................86

Back Bay Clam Chowder......................87

Nantucket Seafood Chowder......................88

Shrimp Bisque......................89

Zuppa di Pesca......................91

Oyster Stew......................92

Newport Harbor Lobster Stew..................93

These recipes can be offered as a main course by doubling the serving size.

Creamy Cold Cucumber Soup

When cukes are overflowing your garden or farm market,
freeze this soup for another season!

Serves 4

2 cups peeled, seeded and
    diced cucumbers

2 teaspoons olive oil

1 tablespoon dill

1 clove garlic, minced

pinch of salt

1 teaspoon white pepper

2¼ cups nonfat sour cream
    and/or plain yogurt

Combine cucumber, olive oil, dill, garlic, salt and pepper. Chill 1 hour, then purée in blender. Fold in yogurt and/or sour cream. Chill at least 4 hours before serving. Garnish with lemon wedges.

Serving: 1/4 recipe	Calories: 136	Protein: 6 gm	Fat Calories: 23
Total Fat: 2.5 gm	Dietary Fiber: 1 gm	Saturated Fat: 0.5 gm	Carbs: 20 gm
Sodium: 157 mg	Fat Component: 17%	Cholesterol: 1 mg	Calcium: 151 mg

Curried Carrot Soup

Choose a curry powder in a color and "heat" to suit your taste.

1 lb. carrots

½ cup chopped onion

2 teaspoons butter

3 cups vegetable broth

½ cup dry brown rice

½ cup nonfat evaporated
  milk

½ teaspoon curry powder

salt and pepper to taste

Serves 4

Peel carrots and chop into 1-inch pieces. In a large pot, sauté onion in butter until clear, but do not brown. Add broth and carrots to pot, and bring to a boil. Reduce heat, add rice and simmer until carrots and rice are tender, about 30 minutes. Purée soup in blender. Return to pot, stir in milk and spices. Warm on medium-low heat, but do not boil.

Serving: 1/4 recipe	Calories: 139	Protein: 8 gm	Fat Calories: 23
Total Fat: 2.5 gm	Dietary Fiber: 4 gm	Saturated Fat: 1 gm	Carbs: 27 gm
Sodium: 176 mg	Fat Component: 16%	Cholesterol: 6 mg	Calcium: 103 mg

Zesty Lentil Stew

Lentil stew is a meal unto itself.

1 lb. dry lentils

8 cups vegetable broth

1 cup chopped onion

1 cup peeled diced carrots

1 cup finely diced celery

2 cloves garlic, minced

1 teaspoon pepper

1 tablespoon cilantro

1 cup peeled, finely
   chopped tomatoes

2 bay leaves

1 tablespoon wine vinegar

Serves 6

Rinse lentils in cold water. Combine all ingredients in large covered pot. Stirring occasionally, slowly simmer for 2 hours, adding water if needed. Discard bay leaves, and adjust seasonings to taste.

Serving: 1/6 recipe	Calories: 337	Protein: 24 gm	Fat Calories: 9
Total Fat: 1 gm	Dietary Fiber: 12 gm	Saturated Fat: 0 gm	Carbs: 62 gm
Sodium: 260 mg	Fat Component: 3%	Cholesterol: 0 mg	Calcium: 86 mg

Home Gardening

Designing, planting and tending a garden is rewarding for your body, spirit and senses. A 10-foot square garden supplies 2 people with produce all summer. Even container gardens and window boxes provide choice selections. For flavor, texture and nutrition – homegrown fruits, vegetables and herbs picked at their prime are beyond comparison. If you're not gardening, participate in an organic co-op, or shop at a farmer's market!

Vegetable Soup with Dumplings

Make your own mixture of roots, leafy greens and vegetables on-the-vine.

5 cups assorted summer
   vegetables, chopped
   into bite-size pieces

1 cup tomato juice

4 cups vegetable broth

1½ cups cake flour

2 teaspoons baking powder

pinch of salt

2 tablespoons fresh herbs

2 eggs

½ cup skim milk

Serves 6

Simmer vegetables in tomato juice on low heat. In a covered pot, warm broth on medium-low heat.

Sift together flour, baking powder and salt. Mix herbs into flour. In a small bowl, whisk eggs with milk, then slowly stir into flour. Batter may be stiff and need a few more drops of milk to form dumplings.

Dip a tablespoon into the simmering broth, form a dumpling in the wet spoon, then lower into the broth. Make all the dumplings, cover, simmer 10 minutes. Add broth and dumplings to vegetable stock.

Serving: 1/6 recipe	Calories: 176	Protein: 5 gm	Fat Calories: 23
Total Fat: 2.5 gm	Dietary Fiber: 8 gm	Saturated Fat: 0 gm	Carbs: 30 gm
Sodium: 376 mg	Fat Component: 13%	Cholesterol: 27 mg	Calcium: 137 mg

Island garden
on Nantucket,
Massachusetts

Hearty Vegetable Minestrone

This is a beautiful soup.

1 cup dried kidney beans

5 cups vegetable broth

3 cups water

2 cups tomato purée

1 leek

1 cup diced onion

1 clove garlic, minced

1 tablespoon olive oil

1 cup shredded cabbage

1 cup chopped carrots

1 cup diced zucchini

1 cup fresh shelled peas

1 cup peeled and chopped
    Italian plum tomatoes

1 tablespoon oregano

¼ cup chopped parsley

1½ cups whole grain elbow
    macaroni

½ cup grated Parmesan
    cheese

Serves 8

Soak kidney beans in cold water at least 2 hours. In a large stockpot, boil beans in broth, water and tomato purée until tender.

Remove green leaves and root tip from leek, wash and dice white stalk. Sauté leek, onion and garlic in olive oil. Add cabbage, carrots and zucchini. Cook 10 minutes over medium heat. Mix cooked vegetables, peas, tomatoes and spices into stockpot.

Bring to a full boil and add macaroni. Reduce heat and gently simmer 30 minutes. Serve soup topped with a tablespoon of grated Parmesan cheese.

Serving: 1/8 recipe	Calories: 274	Protein: 16 gm	Fat Calories: 57
Total Fat: 6 gm	Dietary Fiber: 11 gm	Saturated Fat: 3 gm	Carbs: 43 gm
Sodium: 280 mg	Fat Component: 20%	Cholesterol: 10 mg	Calcium: 220 mg

Cream of Asparagus

A manual food mill produces an exquisite texture.

3 medium-sized potatoes

2 lbs. asparagus

2 leeks, white stalks only

1 cup water

2 cups vegetable broth

¼ teaspoon salt

½ teaspoon white pepper

1 cup skim milk

½ cup nonfat powdered
   milk

Serves 6

Peel and quarter potatoes. Cut dry base ends off asparagus, cut stalks into 1-inch pieces. Separate tip and stalk pieces. Remove green leaves and root tip from leeks, wash and cut into 1-inch pieces. Place potatoes, asparagus stalk pieces, leeks, water and broth in a covered pot. Simmer until potatoes are very soft. Process vegetables and stock through a food mill (or food processor). Whisk in salt, pepper and milks. Add asparagus tips, and warm on low heat for 15 minutes, do not boil.

Serving: 1/6 recipe	Calories: 196	Protein: 15 gm	Fat Calories: 18
Total Fat: 2 gm	Dietary Fiber: 7 gm	Saturated Fat: 0 gm	Carbs: 41 gm
Sodium: 88 mg	Fat Component: 9%	Cholesterol: 0 mg	Calcium: 98 mg

Northend Lobster Bouillabaisse

Stock can conveniently be made by dissolving fish bouillon cubes.

2 teaspoons olive oil

1 cup chopped onion

2 cloves garlic, crushed

2 tablespoons blanched
  almond slivers, crushed

2 celery stalks, chopped

1 cup peeled, seeded and
  diced plum tomatoes

3 tablespoons fresh parsley

1 bay leaf

½ teaspoon thyme

2 cups fish stock

2 cups dry white wine

3 cups cooked lobster meat,
  cut into bite-size pieces

Serves 4

Heat olive oil in a large saucepan. Sauté onion, garlic, almonds and celery. When onions are clear, add tomatoes, parsley, bay leaf, thyme, fish stock and wine. Bring to a boil, slowly simmer 20 minutes. Add lobster 5 minutes before serving to heat through.

Serving: 1/4 recipe	Calories: 274	Protein: 24 gm	Fat Calories: 45
Total Fat: 5 gm	Dietary Fiber: 6 gm	Saturated Fat: 1 gm	Carbs: 10 gm
Sodium: 584 mg	Fat Component: 16%	Cholesterol: 78 mg	Calcium: 126 mg

The Best Lobsters in the World

The East Coast, or Maine Lobster is prized throughout the world for its delectably sweet meat. From Long Island Sound to the Bay of Fundy, thousands of seasonal lobstermen head to sea to set and harvest traps. As lobsters relocate from deep-water winter homes to summer shedding areas, traps are moved closer to shore. Lobsters shed their shells as they grow. New-shelled lobsters are "shedders" or "soft-shells." They contain more water (to expand the shell for growth), but are reputed to be sweeter. Hard-shells have more meat for their size, but cost more per pound. Simply steamed or recipe prepared, Maine lobsters are a welcome feast.

Quick Gazpacho

For a take-out lunch, this tangy summer soup will stay cold in a thermos.

1 cup peeled, seeded and finely diced cucumber

2 cups peeled, seeded and finely diced tomatoes

1 cup vegetable broth

1 cup crushed tomatoes

2 tablespoons diced pimientos

2 teaspoons olive oil

½ cup grated red pepper

½ cup grated green pepper

¼ cup grated red onion

2 tablespoons chives

1 tablespoon fresh dill

pinch of cayenne

salt and pepper to taste

Serves 4

Combine half of the cucumber, tomatoes, vegetable broth, crushed tomatoes and pimientos in blender. Process a minute. Add olive oil and process briefly.

Pour into a bowl, and stir in remaining ingredients. Chill well before serving.

Serving: 1/4 recipe	Calories: 90	Protein: 3 gm	Fat Calories: 27
Total Fat: 3 gm	Dietary Fiber: 3 gm	Saturated Fat: 0.5 gm	Carbs: 15 gm
Sodium: 250 mg	Fat Component: 30%	Cholesterol: 0 mg	Calcium: 43 mg

An incredibly lovely lawn for a picnic
in Coventry, Rhode Island

Back Bay Clam Chowder

Steamer and hen clams are used in New England chowders.
Any fresh local clams are preferable, but even canned clams will do.

1 onion, chopped

1 clove garlic, minced

2 teaspoons butter

2 tablespoons flour

3 cups clam juice or
    fish stock

2 large potatoes, diced

2 cups skim milk blended
    with 1 cup nonfat
    powdered milk

2 cups steamed, shucked
    and chopped clams

¼ teaspoon pepper

Serves 6

Sauté onion and garlic in butter until clear. Blend in flour, whisk in clam juice. Add potatoes. Simmer until potatoes are tender. Process half the liquid and potatoes in blender, then return to pot. Add milk, clams and pepper. Gently simmer to heat (do not boil). Serve with whole grain or oyster crackers.

Serving: 1/6 recipe	Calories: 159	Protein: 12 gm	Fat Calories: 27
Total Fat: 3 gm	Dietary Fiber: 1 gm	Saturated Fat: 2 gm	Carbs: 19 gm
Sodium: 251 mg	Fat Component: 17%	Cholesterol: 16 mg	Calcium: 267 mg

The Yarmouth Clam Festival is held each July in Yarmouth, Maine. The entire village gets involved in the annual three-day coastal community celebration. This is a huge event in the state, all done for the benefit of 35 non-profit organizations. The Festival features a Clam Parade, old-fashioned kids' games and activities, Clam Shucking Contest, Canoe and Kayak Race, antique and craft exhibits, Pan Fried Steele Drum Band, bagpipe and folk music, fireworks, blueberry pancake breakfast, and lots of clams and lobsters – anyway you like 'em!

Nantucket Seafood Chowder

A medley of favorite seasonal seafoods,
this chowder is a warming meal on blustery rainy days.

2 cloves garlic, minced

1 cup chopped onion

2 teaspoons butter

1¾ cups clam juice

2 cups peeled and diced
   potatoes

½ lb. scallops

1 lb. flounder

1 cup chopped shrimp

3 cups skim milk

½ cup nonfat evaporated
   milk

1 tablespoon parsley

½ teaspoon tarragon

2 pinches nutmeg

salt and pepper to taste

Serves 6

In a large pot, sauté garlic with onion in butter until clear. Add clam juice and potatoes. Cover and simmer until potatoes are tender.

Chop scallops and flounder into bite-size pieces. Add scallops, flounder and shrimp to pot. Bring to a slow simmer for 15 minutes. Reduce heat, and add remaining ingredients. Heat well, but do not boil.

Serving: 1/6 recipe	Calories: 281	Protein: 35 gm	Fat Calories: 27
Total Fat: 3 gm	Dietary Fiber: 2 gm	Saturated Fat: 1.5 gm	Carbs: 27 gm
Sodium: 417 mg	Fat Component: 10%	Cholesterol: 83 mg	Calcium: 259 mg

Shrimp Bisque

This bisque will work equally well with any shellfish.

¾ lb. small peeled shrimp

3 cups skim milk blended with 1 cup nonfat powdered milk

½ cup nonfat evaporated milk

¼ cup grated onion

¼ cup finely diced celery

¼ cup finely diced carrot

1 teaspoon butter

2 tablespoons sherry

3 tablespoons flour

2 tablespoons tomato paste

salt and pepper to taste

Serves 6

Clean and wash shrimp. In a medium pot, whisk milks together, add shrimp and simmer on low heat for 10 minutes.

In a saucepan, sauté onion, celery and carrot in butter until soft, but do not brown. Add sherry, then blend in flour, tomato paste, salt and pepper. Over low heat, whisk in milk and shrimp. Transfer to blender, and process until smooth. Return to pot and heat until thickened, but do not boil.

Serving: 1/6 recipe	Calories: 210	Protein: 24 gm	Fat Calories: 18
Total Fat: 2 gm	Dietary Fiber: 1 gm	Saturated Fat: 1 gm	Carbs: 22 gm
Sodium: 419 mg	Fat Component: 9%	Cholesterol: 118 mg	Calcium: 443 mg

Summer Breezes

Ever wake up to a beautiful day and just want to breathe it in? Then just go! Put out the word for a patio picnic, pack a backpack, rent a canoe or sailboat. Keep it simple - it's not about fancy food - it's living the day in open air and long views. If you take lunch outdoors you'll stay out longer, and the day will be more memorable. Isn't there a place you've been wanting to go but never get to? Make it today!

Upper left: Day sailer off Cape Cod, Mass.
Upper right: Sailing Lake Champlain, Vt.
Lower right: Deer on Cliff Island, Me.
Lower center: Baxter State Park, Me.
Left side pictures: Maine coast

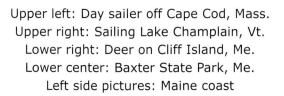

Zuppa di Pesca

Italian immigrants found New England seafood readily adaptable to their traditional dishes. Chill this classic soup for an amazing outdoor lunch.

2 gloves garlic, crushed

½ cup grated red onion

½ cup diced carrot

½ cup diced pepper

½ cup diced celery

½ tablespoon butter

½ tablespoon olive oil

¼ teaspoon ground cloves

½ teaspoon pepper

½ teaspoon oregano

¼ cup fresh parsley

1 cup vermouth

¼ teaspoon Tabasco

¼ cup balsamic vinegar

3 cups plain tomato sauce

5 cups fish or vegetable stock

1 cup dry white wine

36 shellfish (shrimp, clams, mussels, scallops...)

2 lbs. firm ocean fish (salmon, cod, halibut...)

3 whole vegetables (celery, pepper, peeled onion, potato, turnip, carrot...)

Serves 6

In a large saucepan, sauté garlic, onion, carrot, pepper and celery in butter and oil. When tender, mix in spices, vermouth, Tabasco and vinegar. Cook 5 minutes, add tomato sauce and simmer one hour.

Boil stock and wine in a large stockpot. Add seafood and whole vegetables, poach 20 minutes. Remove all seafood with a slotted spoon, cut ocean fish into bite-size pieces, and chill all seafood. Simmer vegetables another hour, then strain. Add strained broth to tomato base, simmer 10 minutes. To serve hot: add seafood, simmer 5 minutes. To serve cold: remove from heat, add seafood, chill.

Serving: 1/6 recipe	Calories: 220	Protein: 20 gm	Fat Calories: 36
Total Fat: 4 gm	Dietary Fiber: 3 gm	Saturated Fat: 0 gm	Carbs: 12 gm
Sodium: 478 mg	Fat Component: 16%	Cholesterol: 64 mg	Calcium: 52 mg

Oyster Stew

In the mid-1800s oyster wagons rolled through New England seaside towns; and "oyster houses" served oysters stewed, spiced, fried, baked, grilled, pickled and fricasseed.

Serves 6

1 tablespoon butter

1 tablespoon sherry

1 tablespoon grated onion

¼ cup diced celery

¼ teaspoon minced garlic

1 tablespoon flour

3 cups skim milk blended with 1 cup nonfat powdered milk

½ cup nonfat evaporated milk

3 cups oysters and their liqueur (see page 48)

salt and pepper to taste

1 tablespoon parsley

Warm butter and sherry in a medium pot over low heat. Add onion, celery and garlic, and sauté until onion clears. Whisk in flour and milks until smooth.

Add oysters and their liqueur, salt and pepper. Cook, without boiling, until milk is hot and oysters float. Sprinkle parsley over stew. Serve at once, so oysters do not toughen by overcooking.

Serving: 1/6 recipe	Calories: 212	Protein: 19 gm	Fat Calories: 50
Total Fat: 5.5 gm	Dietary Fiber: 0 gm	Saturated Fat: 2 gm	Carbs: 21 gm
Sodium: 350 mg	Fat Component: 23%	Cholesterol: 78 mg	Calcium: 416 mg

Eastern oysters of New England are large and flavorful, up to 7 inches long in irregular oval shapes. They are harvested in intertidal zones of rivers and estuaries, at up to 40 feet deep.

Like all seafood, only purchase oysters without any trace of ammonia or strong fishy smell. If freshness is in doubt, ask when the fish market's next delivery will arrive.

To prepare oysters in the shell, see page 48.

Fresh shelled oysters should be plump, creamy in color, with clear liquid (liqueur). If fresh shelled oyster meat is available, this is the way to go. Canned oysters are easier to use, but are smaller and their flavor is not as full.

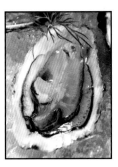

Newport Harbor Lobster Stew

The finest kind!

Serves 6

3 lobsters, steamed

1 clove garlic, crushed

2 teaspoons butter

¼ cup cognac

4 cups fish or vegetable
  broth

1 cup dry white wine

1 teaspoon white pepper

1 cup skim milk

½ cup light cream

salt to taste

Shell lobsters, reserving tail shells. Leave claws whole, but cut other meat into bite-size pieces.

In a large saucepan, sauté garlic in butter. Add cognac, broth, wine, pepper and lobster tail shells. Gently simmer until liquid is reduced by ⅓ (about 3½ cups remaining). Cool 5 minutes, then discard lobster shells. Stir in milk, cream and salt, return to low heat, but do not boil. Five minutes before serving, add lobster meat to warm in stew. Use a slotted spoon to select and divide lobster meat among bowls, then ladle liquid on top.

Serving: 1/6 recipe	Calories: 254	Protein: 31 gm	Fat Calories: 54
Total Fat: 6 gm	Dietary Fiber: 0 gm	Saturated Fat: 2 gm	Carbs: 3 gm
Sodium: 497 mg	Fat Component: 21%	Cholesterol: 90 mg	Calcium: 88 mg

Main Meal Dishes

Brandied Shrimp Scampi.............................95

Mussels in Vermouth Sauce.........................96

Skewered Braised Scallops.........................97

Char-Blackened Bluefish............................99

Cognac Creamed Crab.............................100

Elegant Lobster Pie...............................101

How to Steam Lobsters............................101

Lobster Bake at Sunset............................102

Simply Sole.......................................104

Flounder Florentine...............................105

Halibut with Parsley Sauce.......................106

Codfish Cakes.....................................107

Poached Salmon with Dill Sauce................109

Maple-Mustard Salmon...........................110

Oven-Fried Swordfish.............................111

New England Pot Pie..............................112

Seafood Newburg.................................113

Brandied Shrimp Scampi

Serve on a bed of fettuccine or rice.
Brandied Shrimp Scampi always collects compliments!

Serves 4

¼ cup sesame seeds

2 teaspoons butter

2 teaspoons olive oil

3 cloves garlic, pressed

4 scallions, white part only, finely chopped

1½ lbs. large shrimp, peeled and deveined

2 teaspoons lemon juice

3 tablespoons brandy

salt and pepper to taste

In a large dry skillet over medium heat, shake pan to dry-roast sesame seeds until golden. Set aside.

Heat butter and olive oil in skillet, add garlic and scallions. Dry shrimp in a towel. Raise heat to medium-high, and toss in shrimp. Shake and toss shrimp in pan to sear on all sides.

Before removing from heat, sprinkle with lemon juice and brandy. Allow liquid to evaporate, and the flavors will remain. Toss with salt and pepper. Sprinkle toasted sesame seeds on each serving.

Serving: 1/4 recipe	Calories: 201	Protein: 22 gm	Fat Calories: 54
Total Fat: 6 gm	Dietary Fiber: 0 gm	Saturated Fat: 1.5 gm	Carbs: 8 gm
Sodium: 616 mg	Fat Component: 27%	Cholesterol: 52 mg	Calcium: 74 mg

Mussels in Vermouth Sauce

A coastal specialty.

6 dozen mussels

2 cups water

1-2 cloves garlic, crushed

¼ teaspoon olive oil

2 teaspoons flour

¼ cup vermouth

1 egg yolk, beaten

¼ teaspoon pepper

¼ cup chopped parsley

Serves 4

Scrub mussels and discard any that do not close or have broken shells. Boil water, add mussels, cover and steam until mussels open, about 10 minutes. Pour liquid through a fine mesh to remove sand, reserving 1 cup. Cool mussels, shuck, remove beards, and reserve half of the shells.

In a saucepan, sauté garlic in olive oil. Stir in flour, and brown slightly. Pour in vermouth and reserved cup of cooking liquid. Whisk in egg yolk and pepper. Cook down until the consistency of heavy cream.

Place reserved shells in a large skillet, and mussels inside shells. Drizzle vermouth sauce over mussels, sprinkle with parsley, cover and warm on low heat.

Serving: 1/4 recipe	Calories: 261	Protein: 16 gm	Fat Calories: 63
Total Fat: 7 gm	Dietary Fiber: 2 gm	Saturated Fat: 4.5 gm	Carbs: 28 gm
Sodium: 420 mg	Fat Component: 24%	Cholesterol: 103 mg	Calcium: 120 mg

Skewered Braised Scallops

Compatible with any wine and summer vegetable.
(Shown on the front cover with grilled portobellas and red bell peppers.)

1½ lbs. good-size scallops

Serves 4

Baste #1:

3 tablespoons miso paste

1 tablespoons lemon juice

3 tablespoons dry red wine

Baste #2:

2 teaspoons Worcestershire sauce

1 tablespoon lemon juice

1 tablespoon flour

¼ cup dry white wine

Preheat broiler or light fire in grill. Rinse and dry scallops. If very large, halve, keeping round shape.

In a small saucepan over low heat, whisk choice of baste until thick, but still spreadable. Place scallops on flat skewers, with space between each. Baste.

Broiler method: Rest ends of skewers on rim of deep baking pan (so scallops do not touch pan, but drippings are caught). Broil on middle rack. Turn scallops to brown on all sides, basting as needed. Scallops will cook in 10-12 minutes.

Grilling method: Place skewers on grill over fire that has burned down to hot coals. Turn and baste frequently until seared on all sides.

Serving: 1/4 recipe	Calories: 163	Protein: 29 gm	Fat Calories: 18
Total Fat: 2 gm	Dietary Fiber: 0 gm	Saturated Fat: 0 gm	Carbs: 6 gm
Sodium: 431 mg	Fat Component: 11%	Cholesterol: 56 mg	Calcium: 44 mg

Plymouth Harbor,
Massachusetts

Atlantic Bay
Scallops

Outdoor Grilling

What makes grilling so flavorful? Within a few inches of high heat the outside of food is seared while the juices are concentrated inside. The outer layer of carbohydrates is also broken down, browning and enhancing the exterior. A fire's intense heat can only be sustained for a brief time before meat and fish dry out. Basting sauces extend time on the grill, allowing the interior to finish cooking. Hardwood charcoal made from oak, maple, cherry, apple, hickory, mesquite or alder impart natural aromas. (Avoid standard briquets, they may contain a smelly petroleum base.) To keep delicate vegetables from falling through the grill, use a hinged grilling basket.

From upper left: barbecued kabobs, grilled swordfish,
grilled scallops and portobellas, grilled shrimp, roasted zucchini,
mixed potatoes, Caesar with grilled salmon, corn on the cob, grilled peach à la mode.

Char-Blackened Bluefish

Any firm-fleshed fish is excellent on the grill.
Bluefish is dense; other types of fish may require less cooking time.

4 bluefish or tuna steaks,
   sized to suit appetites

1 cup nonfat mayonnaise

1 tablespoon paprika

1 tablespoon lemon juice

1 teaspoon olive oil

pinch of celery salt

1 teaspoon pepper

Serves 4

Build fire and let it burn down to hot coals. Lower rack to about 2 inches above coals. Pat fish dry.

Blend together mayonnaise, paprika, lemon juice, olive oil, celery salt and pepper.

Thinly coat 1 side of fillets with basting sauce. Place basted side down on the grill. Coat upper side with a thick layer of sauce. Grill 4 minutes, then flip. Baste upper side with a thick layer of sauce. When grilling side is blackened, flip to blacken other side.

Serving: 1/4 recipe	Calories: 162	Protein: 17 gm	Fat Calories: 45
Total Fat: 5 gm	Dietary Fiber: 0 gm	Saturated Fat: 1 gm	Carbs: 10 gm
Sodium: 491 mg	Fat Component: 28%	Cholesterol: 50 mg	Calcium: 11 mg

Cognac Creamed Crab

This is a wonderful dish to serve on a bed of white aromatic rice.

4 cups cooked aromatic rice

Serves 4

Start cooking enough rice to yield 4 cooked cups.

Vegetables:

1 teaspoon butter

½ cup dry white wine

1½ cups julienned carrots cut into 2" lengths

1½ cups julienned red bell pepper cut into 2" lengths

1½ cups thin asparagus cut into 2" lengths

In a medium saucepan, melt butter in wine. Add julienned vegetables, cover and steam on low heat.

For sauce, sauté shallots and garlic in butter until clear. Blend in flour, then cognac, stock and nutmeg. In a separate pot, dissolve powdered milk in cold skim milk, scald, then pour into sauce. Remove from heat, whisk in yolks. Return to medium heat and whisk while sauce thickens to desired creamy consistency. Fold in crab meat to warm for 4 minutes.

Sauce:

2 shallots, finely diced

1 clove garlic, crushed

2 teaspoons butter

2 tablespoons flour

2 tablespoons cognac

½ cup fish stock or clam juice

¼ teaspoon nutmeg

½ cup nonfat powdered milk

1 cup skim milk

2 egg yolks, beaten

1 lb. fresh crab meat

Make a bed of rice on each plate. Place vegetables on the rice, spoon crab sauce on top. Garnish with fresh parsley or tarragon sprigs.

Serving: 1/4 recipe	Calories: 222	Protein: 27 gm	Fat Calories: 59
Total Fat: 6.5 gm	Dietary Fiber: 0 gm	Saturated Fat: 2 gm	Carbs: 10 gm
Sodium: 384 mg	Fat Component: 26%	Cholesterol: 176 mg	Calcium: 231 mg

Aromatic rice is a generic name for varieties with a perfumed nutty scent. Aromatics are available as both brown and white rice. Cooking ratio is 2 cups boiling water to 1 cup dry rice. Varieties have different yields, so check the package for the amount to start with. The brown and long grains also need extended cooking times. Well-known aromatic varieties in the U.S. include American long grain, basmati and jasmine rice.

Elegant Lobster Pie

Lazyman's lobster (shelling it for someone else) is a kindness unto itself. This lobster pie takes your gift to the next level.

Serves 4

4 steamed lobsters

2 shallots, finely diced

2 teaspoons melted butter

1 cup vermouth

1 cup vegetable broth

¼ teaspoon white pepper

3 tablespoons light cream

1¼ cups plain bread crumbs

2 teaspoons canola oil

Remove meat from lobsters, and reserve tail shells. Cut meat into bite-size pieces. Place in a towel and gently pat to remove some of the moisture.

In a large pan, sauté shallots in butter. When clear, add vermouth, broth, pepper and reserved tail shells. Cover pan, and steam on low heat until liquid is reduced to about ¾ cup. Discard lobster shells, stir in cream. Add lobster meat to heat through.

Mix bread crumbs with canola oil. Arrange meat in 4 individual casserole dishes, pour on sauce and sprinkle with crumbs. Broil on middle rack until lightly browned. Do not overcook or lobster will toughen.

Serving: 1/4 recipe	Calories: 286	Protein: 31 gm	Fat Calories: 68
Total Fat: 7.5 gm	Dietary Fiber: 0 gm	Saturated Fat: 3 gm	Carbs: 10 gm
Sodium: 640 mg	Fat Component: 24%	Cholesterol: 112 mg	Calcium: 115 mg

How to Steam Lobsters

Place lobsters in the freezer 10 minutes to numb them. In a 4-5 gallon covered enamel pot over high heat, boil 1-1½ inches of water with 1 tablespoon sea salt. Place lobsters in pot and cover. When water returns to a rolling boil, reduce heat to medium-high and steam another 15 minutes if lobsters are under 1½ pounds each, or 20 minutes if they weigh 1½-2 pounds each. (A 5 gallon pot will hold up to 6 large lobsters.)

Lobster Bake at Sunset

Choose a gravel or sandy area, and start preparations mid-afternoon.
You'll be rewarded at sunset with these gifts from the sea.
(All the fixings can also steam together on a stove top for 40 minutes.)

6 dozen steamer clams

Serves 6

rinsed seaweed, or
   1 head iceberg lettuce

6 potatoes wrapped in
   two layers of foil

6 live lobsters, 1½ lbs. each

6 ears of corn, husked

2-3 cups dry white wine,
   lemon juice and butter

Bring along:
24-quart covered steamer,
shovel, long tongs, safe mitts,
covered campfire pan,
lobster crackers and picks,
corn and potato fixings,
sturdy plates and utensils.

Before leaving: Scrub clams and discard any with broken shells or that do not close tightly when handled. Tie by the dozen in mesh cooking bags or cheesecloth squares, with space for them to open.

Dig a hole at least 3' wide by 30" deep in sand or gravel. Build a driftwood fire in hole, let it die down to hot coals, then level with shovel. Make a 2"-deep bed of seaweed or lettuce in pot, add 6 cups sea or salt water, set on coal and cover. Use tongs to place potatoes on hot coals. Flip potatoes in 30 minutes.

When water boils, put in lobsters and corn. Add a 2" layer of seaweed or lettuce, and clam bags on top. Cover, steam one hour. Carefully unpack pot, then remove from hole. Put wine-butter ingredients in covered pan, warm on embers. Use tongs to retrieve baked potatoes. Shoo new-found "friendly" admirers far away. (Refill fire-pit hole before leaving.)

Serving: 1/6 recipe	Calories: 429	Protein: 53 gm	Fat Calories: 59
Total Fat: 6.5 gm	Dietary Fiber: 5 gm	Saturated Fat: 0.5 gm	Carbs: 48 gm
Sodium: 690 mg	Fat Component: 14%	Cholesterol: 208 mg	Calcium: 147 mg

On the beach at sunset,
Gooseberry Island,
Westport, Massachusetts.

How to Eat a Lobster

Be casual.
(There is no empathy for dramatic episodes involving wine-butter dripping down silk attire, having been preceded by a mouthful of lobster tail.)

Pleasurable moaning and sucking sounds are not always impolite at the table.

If you can't endure messy, don't watch (or comment upon) anyone else's happy meal skills.

With each bite, savor the flavor!

Twist off legs. Break off pincers. Bend or use crackers to separate knuckles.

Use pick and crackers to get meat from legs, claws and pincers. Twist tail from body.

Bend back flippers to break off (meat inside). Peel back upper tail section, pick out gray cord, and any red material. Advanced shelling: ask a local how to get out the body meat.

Simply Sole

What I love about this recipe is everything. It is how to honor fresh fish.
Double the recipe to enjoy fish sandwiches tomorrow.

2 teaspoons butter

1 tablespoon canola oil

1 egg

¼ cup skim milk

½ cup unbleached flour

¼ cup cornmeal

salt and pepper to taste

1½ lbs. fillets of sole or
    flounder

1 teaspoon lemon juice

Serves 4

Over medium heat, warm butter and oil in nonstick
pan. Beat egg with milk in shallow wide bowl. Blend
flour, cornmeal, salt and pepper in a plate. Dredge
fillets in flour, dip in egg-milk mixture, then dredge
in flour again. Fry on both sides. Drain on paper
towels, then sprinkle with lemon juice.

Serving: 1/4 recipe	Calories: 252	Protein: 42 gm	Fat Calories: 68
Total Fat: 7.5 gm	Dietary Fiber: 0 gm	Saturated Fat: 2 gm	Carbs: 1 gm
Sodium: 225 mg	Fat Component: 27%	Cholesterol: 120 mg	Calcium: 42 mg

Flounder Florentine

Flounder and sole are interchangeable. Both are high in protein, selenium, phosphorous, magnesium, B6 and B12, and low in saturated fat.
These are good-for-you fish!

Serves 4

1½ lbs. flounder fillets

1 lb. fresh baby spinach

2 teaspoons butter

2 tablespoons dry white wine

¼ cup grated onion

1 clove garlic, pressed

2 tablespoons flour

1 cup skim milk blended
   with ½ cup nonfat
   powdered milk

1 tablespoon parsley

¼ teaspoon Worcestershire
   sauce

pinch each of dry mustard,
   paprika and nutmeg

¾ cup shredded Gruyère
   or Parmesan cheese

Poach the flounder fillets by steaming them over boiling water until springy to the touch. Wash spinach and remove stems. Steam just until wilted. Place spinach in a sieve, press out liquid.

In a saucepan, melt butter in wine, then sauté grated onion and garlic. Blend in flour, whisk in blended milk and spices, stirring constantly until creamy and smooth. Mix in cheese.

Preheat oven to 350º. Spread spinach in nonstick baking dish, arrange fillets on spinach, pour sauce over all. Bake 15 minutes. Serve at once.

Serving: 1/4 recipe	Calories: 329	Protein: 50 gm	Fat Calories: 50
Total Fat: 5.5 gm	Dietary Fiber: 3 gm	Saturated Fat: 1 gm	Carbs: 15 gm
Sodium: 386 mg	Fat Component: 15%	Cholesterol: 118 mg	Calcium: 329 mg

Mystic, Connecticut is a famous sea-faring town. The Mystic Seaport Museum is also a living maritime historical center. Offering hands-on sailing cruises, marine mammal encounters (Pet-A-Penguin), sea exploration exhibits, joint fishery research and preservation programs. Flatfish studies include flounder species and are conducted by scientists working in cooperation with the museum.

Halibut with Parsley Sauce

Haddock is now prevalent on Georges Bank, and easier to find at market.

Serves 4

1 cup water

1 cup wine

1½ lbs. fresh halibut
   or haddock

1 teaspoon melted butter

2 teaspoons olive oil

2 cloves garlic, halved

1 tablespoon flour

¾ cup nonfat buttermilk

½ teaspoon white pepper

¼ teaspoon salt

3 tablespoons parsley

1 teaspoon lemon zest

¼ teaspoon lemon juice

Boil water and wine in a covered pot. Carefully lower fish into pot and steam just until fish is opaque all the way through. Remove from heat, but keep warm in covered pot. Reserve 1 cup of fish broth.

In a saucepan, heat olive oil with garlic. When garlic has browned, stir, and remove it from oil. Over medium heat, blend flour into oil. Whisk in 1 cup fish broth, stirring until thick and smooth. Mix in buttermilk, white pepper, salt and parsley. When hot, remove from heat and stir in lemon zest and juice. Spoon sauce over poached halibut. Garnish with fresh herbs and capers.

Serving: 1/4 recipe	Calories: 227	Protein: 36 gm	Fat Calories: 63
Total Fat: 7 gm	Dietary Fiber: 0 gm	Saturated Fat: 1 gm	Carbs: 3 gm
Sodium: 237 mg	Fat Component: 28%	Cholesterol: 57 mg	Calcium: 89 mg

Codfish Cakes

Prepared in the traditional fashion of native Portuguese.

1 lb. salt codfish

3 cups water

1 large carrot, quartered

1 onion, quartered

1 celery stalk, quartered

1 garlic clove, halved

1 bay leaf

3 medium-size potatoes,
    quartered

1 teaspoon lemon zest

¼ cup grated onion

1 teaspoon pepper

1 egg

1 tablespoon skim milk

2 tablespoons flour

2 tablespoons canola oil

Serves 4

Soak salted codfish in cold water for 6 hours, pounding out, rinsing and changing water every hour to remove the salt.

Boil 3 cups water with carrot, onion, celery, garlic, bay leaf and potatoes. Simmer 15 minutes. Tie codfish in a cheesecloth and simmer 5 minutes in the broth. Remove pot from heat, leaving fish in hot broth 10 minutes more, then remove codfish and pat dry. Return pot to heat and continue cooking until potatoes are tender.

Put codfish in bowl, use two forks to flake into shreds. Place potatoes in a separate bowl and mash. Combine potatoes, lemon zest, onion, pepper, egg, milk and flour with codfish. Form into small oval cakes. Heat oil in nonstick frying pan over medium-high heat, fry cakes on both sides until browned.

Serving: 1/4 recipe	Calories: 325	Protein: 32 gm	Fat Calories: 81
Total Fat: 9 gm	Dietary Fiber: 5 gm	Saturated Fat: 1 gm	Carbs: 30 gm
Sodium: 415 mg	Fat Component: 25%	Cholesterol: 116 mg	Calcium: 77 mg

Salmon

Atlantic salmon are world travelers. After a few years in the river, they change into saltwater fish. Swimming thousands of miles, salmon traverse the North Atlantic from the U.S. to Russia's White Sea. This fish is an excellent source of protein, Vitamin D, B6, B12, niacin, selenium and omega-3 fatty acids; protecting against heart disease and diabetes. Salmon is a super-food; available fresh, frozen, canned, hot (dry) and cold (moist) smoked. Wild-caught is preferred over farm-raised, which may have contaminants. Before cooking, feel for bones and remove with pliers.

Clockwise from top left: Cold smoked salmon platter, broiled BBQ salmon, fresh steaks, poached fillet, fresh fillet strips, salmon skewers on the grill, Atlantic salmon being released, a classic full-dress salmon fly, and raw sushi-style salmon salad.

Poached Salmon with Dill Sauce

Fresh dill is a weed; it's easy to grow or find in the produce section.

1½ lbs. fresh salmon fillets

1½ cups dry white wine

1 teaspoon butter

2 teaspoons flour

1 teaspoon white pepper

2 tablespoons fresh dill

1 tablespoon lemon juice

pinch of cayenne

pinch of salt

Serves 4

Cut salmon fillets into 4 equal portions. In a large saucepan, bring white wine to a simmer. Place fillets in saucepan, cover. Poach 12 minutes, or until the inner flesh is light pink. Remove salmon with slotted spatula, cover and place in preheated 250º oven.

Combine poaching liquid in blender with remaining ingredients, and process 1 minute. Return to saucepan, and whisk until thickened. Serve poached salmon fillets with dill sauce spooned on top.

Serving: 1/4 recipe	Calories: 275	Protein: 34 gm	Fat Calories: 63
Total Fat: 7 gm	Dietary Fiber: 0 gm	Saturated Fat: 1.5 gm	Carbs: 2 gm
Sodium: 155 mg	Fat Component: 23%	Cholesterol: 91 mg	Calcium: 21 mg

Maple-Mustard Salmon

Maple syrup and mustard are delightful contrasts glazed on fresh salmon.

Serves 4

2 tablespoons Dijon
   mustard

¼ cup maple syrup

1 teaspoon lemon juice

½ teaspoon white pepper

pinch of salt

1½ lbs. fresh salmon fillets

1 teaspoon melted butter

Preheat broiler. Blend mustard, maple syrup, lemon juice, pepper and salt.

Place fillets on nonstick broiler pan, and set 6 inches under broiler for 4 minutes. Remove and flip fillets. Brush with butter and coat with maple-mustard sauce. Return to broiler, leaving oven door tipped open. Salmon is done when inner flesh is light pink. Serve with juices from pan spooned over fish.

Serving: 1/4 recipe	Calories: 257	Protein: 34 gm	Fat Calories: 63
Total Fat: 7 gm	Dietary Fiber: 0 gm	Saturated Fat: 1.5 gm	Carbs: 13 gm
Sodium: 152 mg	Fat Component: 25%	Cholesterol: 91 mg	Calcium: 32 mg

Searsport, Maine

Oven-Fried Swordfish

Swordfish releases oil as it cooks, allowing the
egg white and flour breading to bake into a crispy coating.

Serves 4

1 tablespoon olive oil

1½ lbs. swordfish steaks

2 egg whites

¾ cup flour

1 teaspoon pepper

pinch of salt

1 teaspoon garlic powder

Preheat oven to 400º. Trim fatty and any tough-looking areas from fish. Pat dry. In a shallow pan, beat egg whites. Place swordfish into whites, flip to coat. Mix flour and spices in a plate. Dredge steaks in flour mixture. Set on nonstick pan to bake, flipping after bottom side has browned. Swordfish is ready as soon as steaks are opaque all the way through.

Serving: 1/4 recipe	Calories: 289	Protein: 27 gm	Fat Calories: 54
Total Fat: 6 gm	Dietary Fiber: 1 gm	Saturated Fat: 2 gm	Carbs: 14 gm
Sodium: 207 mg	Fat Component: 19%	Cholesterol: 66 mg	Calcium: 13 mg

Ask at the fish counter if they'll trim off
excess fat and dark areas. Our market
will, so we only buy the most desirable
tender swordfish meat.

New England Pot Pie

When your family has a hankering for steaming pot pies, this is it.

Serves 4

¼ cup canola oil

2½ cups all-purpose flour

½ cup ice water

2 eggs, beaten

20 small pearl onions

½ cup chopped celery

1 teaspoon butter

3 tablespoons flour

2 teaspoons thyme

1 cup vegetable broth

1 cup skim milk blended
  with ½ cup nonfat
  powdered milk

1 cup frozen corn kernels

1 cup peas

3 cups bite-size pieces
  cooked fish, shellfish,
  tofu or white meat

1 teaspoon skim milk

Cut ¼ cup oil into flour with pastry cutter or knives, until mixture resembles texture of peas. Stir in ice water, then eggs. Roll between floured sheets of waxed paper to make top and bottom crusts for 4 small ovenproof bowls. Set bottom crusts in bowls.

Peel and halve pearl onions, sauté with celery in butter. Stir in 3 tablespoons flour and thyme. Slowly whisk in vegetable broth and milk. Simmer until thickened. Add corn, peas, fish, tofu or meat. Pour into pie bowls, and cover with top crusts. Pinch and flute edges together. Brush top with milk, and make 5 slits in each top with knife. Bake at 350° for 35 minutes, or until golden brown.

Serving: 1/4 recipe	Calories: 444	Protein: 42 gm	Fat Calories: 86
Total Fat: 9.5 gm	Dietary Fiber: 9 gm	Saturated Fat: 2.5 gm	Carbs: 43 gm
Sodium: 312 mg	Fat Component: 19%	Cholesterol: 257 mg	Calcium: 170 mg

Seafood Newburg

A very impressive dish, with a richness that will be remembered.

Serves 6

1 lb. of any firm white fish

½ lb. shrimp, peeled and deveined

½ lb. small bay scallops

1 teaspoon butter

2 shallots, finely diced

½ cup Madeira

2 cups skim milk blended with 1 cup nonfat powdered milk

3 egg yolks

1 tablespoon tomato paste

salt and white pepper

6 slices toast, halved

Poach fish, shrimp and scallops in boiling water for 8-10 minutes. Drain well.

Heat butter in saucepan. Sauté shallots 5 minutes. Stir in Madeira. Beat milk with egg yolks. Whisk into shallot mixture, stirring constantly while sauce thickens. Add tomato paste, salt and white pepper to taste. Gently fold in fish and heat. Serve Newburg over sliced toast halves.

Serving: 1/6 recipe	Calories: 364	Protein: 45 gm	Fat Calories: 63
Total Fat: 7 gm	Dietary Fiber: 1 gm	Saturated Fat: 2 gm	Carbs: 24 gm
Sodium: 501 mg	Fat Component: 17%	Cholesterol: 241 mg	Calcium: 364 mg

Pasta, Beans and Grains

Providence Primavera............................115

Lasagna with Roasted Bell Peppers............117

Pesto Penne..................................118

Cape Ann Tuna Noodle Casserole..............119

Lobster Ravioli.................... 120

Layered Eggplant Provençal. 122

Zucchini and Shrimp Risotto....................123

Chestnut Stuffing............................124

Rye Berries with Mushrooms 125

Boston Spirited Baked Beans...................127

Bean-Hole Beans..............................128

Baked Stuffed Tomatoes........................129

Whole-grain pasta can be substituted for regular noodles in any recipe.
Whole grains provide protein, fiber and beneficial vitamins.

Providence Primavera

Cool and refreshing on a warm evening.

½ cup purple onion, finely diced

1 cup diced red pepper

1 cup snow peas, cut diagonally into 1" pieces

¼ cup chopped scallions

8 black olives, chopped

6 ripe plum tomatoes, peeled and chopped

½ cup red wine vinegar

2 cups tomato purée

1 tablespoon fresh basil

1 tablespoon oregano

½ teaspoon pepper

2 cloves garlic, minced

2 teaspoons lime zest

1 lb. dry spaghetti pasta

2 teaspoons canola oil

¼ cup grated Parmesan cheese

Serves 4

In a large saucepan, combine vegetables, vinegar, tomato purée, spices and lime zest. Simmer at least an hour, until a small amount put on a plate does not show a rim of liquid separating from sauce. Chill.

Boil pasta just until tender, drain. Toss with oil, cover and chill. When spaghetti and sauce are thoroughly chilled, divide pasta among plates and ladle primavera sauce on top. Sprinkle with Parmesan.

Serving: 1/4 recipe	Calories: 350	Protein: 22 gm	Fat Calories: 63
Total Fat: 7 gm	Dietary Fiber: 10 gm	Saturated Fat: 2 gm	Carbs: 120 gm
Sodium: 422 mg	Fat Component: 18%	Cholesterol: 6 mg	Calcium: 239 mg

The Italian Influence

The Roman Empire became a center of creative cooking when ingredients from across the Empire streamed into Italy. The monks preserved recipes that explained how to use imported exotic ingredients. Later, when Venice and the city-states sent trading ships around the globe, they brought new waves of ingredients back to Italy. Under the influence of the Medici family, the world's first cooking school was opened in Florence in the 14th century. By the time Marco Polo made his historic trip to Asia, pasta had become a household staple. When French cooking first gained acclaim in the 18th century, it was actually based on Italian cooking style and techniques.

At the end of the 19th and early 20th centuries, a huge surge of Italians immigrated to the U.S. Many settled in New England, especially Rhode Island and Boston's North End. With many of those early immigrants coming from the central and southern sections of Italy, it is their cuisine that predominates in the recipes we know as Italian. Boston's North End and Providence, Rhode Island, are both well known for exceptional Italian restaurants.

Lasagna with Roasted Bell Peppers

To control sodium, stock up on unsalted canned tomato products.

Serves 6

2 lbs. bell peppers in assorted colors

1 onion, diced

2 cloves garlic, minced

1 teaspoon olive oil

32 oz. canned Italian-style diced plum tomatoes

1 cup dry white wine

6 oz. can unsalted tomato paste

1 teaspoon each: rosemary, basil, pepper, oregano

1 teaspoon brown sugar

9 ruffled lasagna noodles

1½ cups shredded part-skim mozzarella cheese

Bechamel Sauce:

3 tablespoons flour

1¼ cups skim milk

1 garlic clove, minced

pinch of nutmeg

pinch of pepper

½ cup grated Parmesan cheese

Char peppers in broiler, turning frequently. Place in paper bag 10 minutes, then peel off skins. Seed and cut into 2-inch strips.

In a large saucepan, sauté onion and garlic in oil. Add canned tomatoes and their juice to saucepan with wine, tomato paste, spices and brown sugar. Simmer until liquid is reduced by half.

Boil noodles until tender but firm to the bite. Drain, spread on towels and pat dry.

Sauce: In a saucepan, blend flour with ¼ cup milk, then whisk in remaining milk, garlic and spices. Stirring constantly, simmer 2 minutes. Remove from heat, stir in Parmesan.

Preheat oven to 350º. In a 9" x 12" nonstick baking pan, thinly spread 2 tablespoons of tomato sauce. Make layers of: 3 noodles cut to pan's length, ⅓ of the tomato sauce, ⅓ of the peppers, and dots of ⅓ of the Bechamel Sauce. Repeat layering sequence 2 more times. Bake for 35 minutes, or until piping hot and baked through.

Serving: 1/6 recipe	Calories: 381	Protein: 17 gm	Fat Calories: 63
Total Fat: 7 gm	Dietary Fiber: 7 gm	Saturated Fat: 2 gm	Carbs: 59 gm
Sodium: 378 mg	Fat Component: 17%	Cholesterol: 9 mg	Calcium: 303 mg

Pesto Penne

Balance out the pasta with a large salad or steamed vegetables.

Serves 6

1½ cups packed fresh
  basil leaves

1 tablespoon olive oil

1 tablespoon lemon juice

2 tablespoons pine nuts

1 clove garlic, minced

½ teaspoon white pepper

¼ cup grated Parmesan
  cheese

¼ cup grated Romano
  cheese

1½ lbs. dry penne noodles

With blender running on high speed, carefully drop in basil leaves, olive oil, lemon juice, pine nuts, garlic and pepper. Stop blender as needed to scrape mixture down from sides. Process until well blended. Transfer to a mixing bowl and stir in cheeses.

Boil penne just until tender. Mix 2 tablespoons of boiled water into the pesto sauce. Drain pasta and toss with pesto, or divide penne among plates and spoon pesto on top.

Serving: 1/6 recipe	Calories: 414	Protein: 22 gm	Fat Calories: 99
Total Fat: 11 gm	Dietary Fiber: 4 gm	Saturated Fat: 3 gm	Carbs: 83 gm
Sodium: 132 mg	Fat Component: 24%	Cholesterol: 175 mg	Calcium: 117 mg

Cape Ann Tuna Noodle Casserole

Enrich tuna casserole by poaching previously frozen tuna steaks.

6 cups skim milk

1 lb. dry egg noodles

½ cup chopped onion

2 cloves garlic, minced

1 teaspoon canola oil

1½ cups sliced mushrooms

3 dashes tamari or soy sauce

½ teaspoon pepper

2 cups nonfat sour cream

2 eggs, beaten

1 cup grated part-skim
     mozzarella cheese

18 oz. canned tuna in water

1½ cups cooked peas

Serves 6

Heat milk until gently simmering. Add noodles and cook until tender, but firm to the bite. Drain, reserving 2 cups of the milk.

Sauté onion and garlic in oil. Add mushrooms, cover pan. When mushrooms begin to soften, add reserved milk, tamari or soy sauce, and pepper. Remove from heat, stir in sour cream, eggs and mozzarella. Drain tuna, flake into small pieces. Gently fold tuna, peas and noodles into mixture, then transfer into a nonstick casserole pan. Bake 30 minutes at 350º.

Serving: 1/6 recipe	Calories: 385	Protein: 34 gm	Fat Calories: 63
Total Fat: 7 gm	Dietary Fiber: 3 gm	Saturated Fat: 2 gm	Carbs: 55 gm
Sodium: 393 mg	Fat Component: 16%	Cholesterol: 134 mg	Calcium: 225 mg

Singing Beach
Manchester-by-the-Sea, Massachusetts

This Cape Ann town is famous for the sand on its beach. Pale and soft underfoot, each step elicits a squeak, so a brisk walk becomes music. The beach also has impressive rock outcroppings to climb. Cape Ann is part of the North Shore of Boston. Its protected harbors, inlets and coves created natural ports for development of the fishing industry. Cape Ann today is also a vibrant coastal peninsula – with exquisite homes, lighthouses, excellent seafood restaurants, fishing, whale watching, galleries, music, and of course, beaches!

Lobster Ravioli

Shrimp or crab can be used instead of lobster.

Serves 4

Pasta:

1 cup unbleached flour

1 egg

1 tablespoon beet juice
   (for color) or water

pinch of salt

1 teaspoon canola oil

Sauce:

1 teaspoon butter

1 clove garlic, pressed

1 tablespoon flour

1 cup vegetable broth

½ cup dry white wine

2 teaspoons tomato paste

¼ teaspoon each: nutmeg,
   pepper, chopped parsley

½ cup skim milk

1 cup nonfat sour cream

Filling:

2 cups very finely diced
   lobster meat

¼ cup shredded
   Provolone cheese

½ teaspoon pepper

Combine flour, egg, water, salt and oil with your fingers or in food processor until well blended. Following manufacturer's directions, process into sheets through pasta machine.

Melt butter and sauté garlic. Blend in flour, then whisk in broth, wine, tomato paste and spices. Simmer and whisk until thickened. Reduce heat to low, stir in milk and sour cream.

Mix ½ cup of the sauce with lobster, Provolone and pepper. On a sheet of pasta dough, spoon 1 tablespoon filling (or suitable amount for your crimp), spacing as necessary for cutting. Cover with top sheet, crimp and cut into squares. Boil ravioli 3 minutes in salted water, drain well. Ladle sauce onto each plate, place ravioli on top.

Serving: 1/4 recipe	Calories: 298	Protein: 19 gm	Fat Calories: 72
Total Fat: 8 gm	Dietary Fiber: 2 gm	Saturated Fat: 3.5 gm	Carbs: 36 gm
Sodium: 506 mg	Fat Component: 24%	Cholesterol: 57 mg	Calcium: 185 mg

Homemade ravioli requires a pasta machine and pastry crimper. There are a number of manual and electric machines, rollers, crimpers, cutters, molds and presses. If fresh pasta is your thing, this will be a fun trip to the kitchen store!

Atlantic Puffins

These incredibly cute seabirds nest on a few Maine islands from May to August. Their populations are more concentrated on the Canadian islands north to Newfoundland. September to April is spent far off-shore on the open ocean. At 13" long, adults weigh a pound, but fly at 55 mph! Diving from the air or water's surface, their wings provide fast underwater propulsion. Puffins catch small fish and crustaceans, swallowing them underwater. When feeding chicks, a parent can carry 30 small fish crosswise in its bill. Nests have one egg. For landing tours to Maine's puffin colony on Machias Seal Island, see: www.mainebirding.net/puffin/trips.htm

Layered Eggplant Provençal

Baby gourmet eggplants are not bitter, and do not need to be peeled.
The little purple, white and striped eggplants are elongated or globe-shaped.

6 baby gourmet eggplants
   (or 2 large common)

2 tablespoons canola oil

1½ cups skim milk

3 tablespoons flour

2 egg yolks, beaten

¼ teaspoon garlic powder

salt and pepper to taste

1 cup shredded lowfat
   Swiss Lorraine cheese

3 tablespoons diced shallots

3 cups sliced mushrooms

¼ cup vermouth

1 tablespoon lemon juice

1½ cups tomato sauce

6 cups cooked aromatic rice
   (see page 100)

Serves 6

Cut eggplants lengthwise into ¼-inch-thick slices. (See below.) Toss with 1½ tablespoons oil. Heat a large nonstick frying pan, fry until lightly browned on both sides. Drain on paper towels.

In a saucepan, slowly whisk milk into flour until smooth. Set over moderate heat and beat. Remove from heat and briskly beat in egg yolks, garlic, salt and pepper. Stir in cheese. Return to heat and whisk until thick and smooth.

Sauté shallots and mushrooms in ½ tablespoon oil. Add vermouth and lemon juice, simmer until just a little liquid remains. Fold in ½ cup cheese sauce.

In a 9" x 12" nonstick pan, spread 2 tablespoons tomato sauce. Make 2 sets of layers, each using half of the rice, cheese sauce, mushrooms, eggplant and tomato sauce. (Evenly dab spoonfuls of sauces, don't spread them out.) Bake at 350º for 40 minutes.

Serving: 1/6 recipe	Calories: 255	Protein: 14 gm	Fat Calories: 72
Total Fat: 8 gm	Dietary Fiber: 6 gm	Saturated Fat: 1 gm	Carbs: 38 gm
Sodium: 443 mg	Fat Component: 28%	Cholesterol: 31 mg	Calcium: 182 mg

To take away the bitterness of large common eggplants: peel, slice and "sweat" the slices by generously sprinkling with salt. Drain one hour in a colander. Rinse well to remove salt before using.

Zucchini and Shrimp Risotto

Lusciously smooth.

Serves 6

1 medium onion, diced

½ cup chopped celery

2 cloves garlic, minced

1 tablespoon olive oil

2 cups dry arborio rice

½ cup dry white wine

6 cups vegetable broth

2 cups zucchini slices

1 cup diced red pepper

1 lb. shrimp, peeled and
  deveined

¼ teaspoon saffron

½ teaspoon pepper

2 tablespoons parsley

2 teaspoons butter

½ cup grated Parmesan
  cheese

In a very large saucepan, sauté onion, celery and garlic in oil until onion clears. Stir in rice, then turn heat to high and add white wine. Cook until liquid is reduced by half, then reduce heat to medium.

Heat vegetable broth, and keep it simmering while making risotto. Ladle hot broth into rice, ½ cup at a time. Stir, and allow rice to absorb liquid after each addition. After final addition of broth, add vegetables, shrimp and spices into risotto. Cook 15 minutes more, adding liquid if needed. When rice is soft and creamy, mix in butter and Parmesan.

Serving: 1/6 recipe	Calories: 408	Protein: 9 gm	Fat Calories: 72
Total Fat: 8 gm	Dietary Fiber: 4 gm	Saturated Fat: 2.5 gm	Carbs: 69 gm
Sodium: 314 mg	Fat Component: 18%	Cholesterol: 8 mg	Calcium: 113 mg

Chestnut Stuffing

Stuffing does not need to be "stuffed" to make a good side dish.
This recipe, however, is excellent for stuffing baked fish or shrimp.

Serves 4

1 lb. fresh chestnuts
   (not horse chestnuts)

1 cup chopped onion

½ cup chopped celery

1 tablespoon canola oil

1 teaspoon thyme

1 teaspoon sage

1 tablespoon parsley

salt and pepper to taste

2 cups ½-inch cubes stale
   French or plain bread

1 cup warm skim milk

1 teaspoon lemon zest

With a sharp paring knife, score an "X" in the bottom of chestnuts. Place on cookie sheet in 350º oven and roast until shells are noticeably browned. When cool enough to handle, crack open and chop nut meats.

Sauté chestnut meats, onion and celery in oil. Stir in spices, then bread cubes. Cook until bread cubes start to brown, then slowly pour in milk. Remove from heat and toss in lemon zest. Serve immediately or use for stuffing.

Serving: 1/4 recipe	Calories: 262	Protein: 7 gm	Fat Calories: 45
Total Fat: 5 gm	Dietary Fiber: 6 gm	Saturated Fat: 1 gm	Carbs: 48 gm
Sodium: 203 mg	Fat Component: 17%	Cholesterol: 1 mg	Calcium: 134 mg

Rye Berries with Mushrooms

Rye berries have a sweet nutty aroma.
Any variety of mushroom will be delicious in this recipe.

1 cup rye berries

3½ cups water

2 tablespoons shallots

1 teaspoon canola oil

½ cup chopped mushrooms

1 teaspoon basil

1 teaspoon sage

1 teaspoon chopped parsley

salt and pepper to taste

Serves 4

Wash rye berries. In a covered pot, boil water then add berries. Simmer 1 hour, or until tender.

Sauté shallots in oil. When almost clear, add mushrooms and spices. Cover pan, and turn heat to low. Leave on heat 10 minutes.

When rye berries have absorbed all the water and are soft, combine with mushrooms. Serve hot.

Serving: 1/4 recipe	Calories: 103	Protein: 9 gm	Fat Calories: 9
Total Fat: 1 gm	Dietary Fiber: 1 gm	Saturated Fat: 0 gm	Carbs: 7 gm
Sodium: 36 mg	Fat Component: 9%	Cholesterol: 0 mg	Calcium: 19 mg

New England Vineyards and Wines

About 50 wineries in New England produce an eclectic selection of fruit and grape wines. Massachusetts, Vermont, New Hampshire and Maine focus on fruit wines, although new grape varieties bred to thrive in the climate are now being grown. Fruit is used for sweet dessert wines, and classic dry wines. Northern New England boasts an award-winning dry blueberry, and superb pear, apple and raspberry wines. Connecticut and Rhode Island have distinguished classic wineries, producing quality reds, whites and dessert wines. The Connecticut Wine Trail offers a two-day tasting tour. Most New England vineyards have tasting rooms for sampling and discussing the fine points with the owners: www.oxfordwineroom.com/Vineyards.asp

Boston Spirited Baked Beans

The sap of Vermont, New Hampshire and Maine maple trees is tapped in spring, boiled down, and bottled to stay fresh for over a year. This spicy and sweet dish is not boring baked beans!

2 lbs. dry navy or cannellini beans

1 teaspoon olive oil

2 cups chopped onion

1 clove garlic, minced

1 teaspoon ground ginger

2 cups apple cider

2 cups dry white wine

1 cup water

½ cup maple syrup

½ cup brown sugar

2 teaspoons Dijon mustard

3 bay leaves

½ cup chopped parsley

¼ teaspoon ground cloves

½ teaspoon pepper

¼ teaspoon salt

Serves 12

Wash beans, soak overnight in water, then drain and rinse. In a large covered bean pot, mix together all ingredients, then wipe clean the pot's rim. Bake 3 hours at 350°, adding water if needed. When beans are tender, remove cover and bake 20 minutes. Just before serving, briefly set under broiler to brown.

Serving: 1/12 recipe	Calories: 186	Protein: 17 gm	Fat Calories: 9
Total Fat: 1 gm	Dietary Fiber: 1 gm	Saturated Fat: 0 gm	Carbs: 107 gm
Sodium: 61 mg	Fat Component: 5%	Cholesterol: 0 mg	Calcium: 178 mg

Bean-Hole Beans

The Maine Penobscot Indians cooked most food in covered fire-pit holes. Bean-Hole festivals and suppers are still common old-fashioned gatherings in Maine and New Hampshire.

Serves 12

2 lbs. dry great northern, yellow eye, soldier or Jacob's Ladder beans

1 gallon boiling water or weak vegetable broth

2 cups diced onion

1 cup molasses

1 cup brown sugar

¼ cup spiced mustard

salt and pepper to taste

Note: As you can imagine, an appropriate photo of men digging up beans was not available. Since fire-pit food has such an amazing flavor, pretty pictures of people politely gorging it down were also unavailable. Please feel free to send in Bean-Hole Bean supper photos for the next printing!

Build an outdoor fire in a large square hole, preferably in gravel-type soil. Feed the fire with plenty of wood, so it produces a good amount of hot embers and coals. When the fire has burned down, use a shovel to carefully level the center for the bean pot, and the remaining coals into the corners.

Select a large cast-iron pot with a handle and tight-fitting lid. Mix all ingredients in the pot, cover. Two people can use a long 2" x 4" to lower pot by the handle to rest on coals. (If you can't lower it all the way down, shovel more coals to the center.) Place a wet towel over the pot to keep the ashes out. Shovel remaining coals around the sides and onto top of the pot. Fill in hole with gravel. Leave buried at least 6 hours, then carefully dig up your bean-hole beans!

Serving: 1/12 recipe	Calories: 121	Protein: 10 gm	Fat Calories: 5
Total Fat: 0.5 gm	Dietary Fiber: 2 gm	Saturated Fat: 0 gm	Carbs: 27 gm
Sodium: 269 mg	Fat Component: 4%	Cholesterol: 0 mg	Calcium: 74 mg

The White Mountains of New Hampshire

Baked Stuffed Tomatoes

When there are big red beauties on the vine,
it's time for Baked Stuffed Tomatoes!

4 large beefsteak tomatoes

1 teaspoon canola oil

2 tablespoons chopped
   scallions

½ cup finely diced celery

1 clove crushed garlic

1 cup diced yellow squash

2 tablespoons chopped
   parsley

¼ teaspoon salt

½ teaspoon pepper

1½ cups cooked brown rice,
   millet or other grain

Serves 4

Cut large hollows in the stem end of tomatoes, being careful not to cut a hole in the bottoms. Scoop out most of the seeds and pulp. Invert tomatoes on a rack and drain 15 minutes.

Heat oil and sauté scallion, celery and garlic. Add yellow squash, cover pan and cook 10 minutes. Drain off liquid, add spices and grain. Stuff tomatoes.

Preheat oven to 350º. Select a baking pan in which the tomatoes can be tightly placed side-by-side. Pour ½ cup water into pan, then arrange tomatoes. Bake 20 minutes; remove with slotted spoon.

Serving: 1/4 recipe	Calories: 75	Protein: 10 gm	Fat Calories: 14
Total Fat: 1.5 gm	Dietary Fiber: 5 gm	Saturated Fat: 0.5 gm	Carbs: 11 gm
Sodium: 151 mg	Fat Component: 18%	Cholesterol: 0 mg	Calcium: 33 mg

Vegetables and Sauces

Carrot-Beet Julienne....................................131

Broccoli with Lemon Butter.....................132

Mixed Steamed Greens...........................132

Herbed Cauliflower.................................133

Fresh Roasted Corn................................135

Savory Succotash...................................135

Zucchini Hash Browns.............................136

Mushroom Quiche...................................137

Roasted Asiago Peas...............................138

Quick Stir-Fry Asparagus..........................140

Artichoke Florentine................................141

Spinach Frittata.....................................142

Spicy Roasted Potatoes...........................143

Chilled Green Beans................................145

Rutabaga Mash......................................146

Onion Pie au Gratin................................147

Carrot-Beet Julienne

A contrast of colors and taste, vibrantly sweet and tangy.

½ cup water

2 cups carrots, peeled and diagonally cut into strips

2 cups beets, peeled and diagonally cut into strips

1 tablespoon honey

2 tablespoons orange juice

1 teaspoon butter

1 teaspoon vinegar

pinch of salt

½ teaspoon lemon juice

1 teaspoon chopped parsley

Serves 4

In a saucepan, boil water over medium-high heat. Add all ingredients, except parsley. Simmer until water evaporates, about 10 minutes. Remove from heat, stir to coat. Sprinkle with parsley.

Serving: 1/4 recipe	Calories: 96	Protein: 2 gm	Fat Calories: 9
Total Fat: 1 gm	Dietary Fiber: 6 gm	Saturated Fat: 1 gm	Carbs: 20 gm
Sodium: 145 mg	Fat Component: 9%	Cholesterol: 3 mg	Calcium: 37 mg

View from the lawn at
Jordan Pond House Restaurant,
Acadia National Park, Maine.

Broccoli with Lemon Butter

1 large head broccoli
1 teaspoon butter
1 teaspoon olive oil
¼ cup dry white wine
1 teaspoon lemon juice
salt and pepper to taste

Serves 4

Cut broccoli into florets and place in steamer over boiling water. Steam about 7 minutes, until dark green and tender. Do not overcook.

While broccoli is cooking, melt butter with remaining ingredients in a very small saucepan. Drain broccoli. Pour lemon butter over broccoli florets. Serve hot.

Serving: 1/4 recipe	Calories: 69	Protein: 4 gm	Fat Calories: 23
Total Fat: 2.5 gm	Dietary Fiber: 4 gm	Saturated Fat: 1 gm	Carbs: 3 gm
Sodium: 79 mg	Fat Component: 33%	Cholesterol: 3 mg	Calcium: 49 mg

Mixed Steamed Greens

½ cup chopped onion
1 clove garlic, minced
1 tablespoon butter
¼ cup dry white wine
1 bay leaf
4 packed cups chopped
    mixed greens: mustard
    greens, kale, spinach,
    beet and collard greens
salt and pepper to taste

Serves 4

In a large saucepan, sauté onion and garlic in butter and wine for 4 minutes. Add bay leaf, cover pan. Wash and chop greens before measuring. Add greens to saucepan, cover and steam. Stir occasionally.

Cook greens until they are the texture you like. I like them lightly wilted, but others prefer completely cooked down. Less cooking preserves vitamins. When ready to serve: drain liquid, discard bay leaf, add salt and pepper to taste. This technique retains a buttery flavor, although most of the fat drains off.

Serving: 1/4 recipe	Calories: 93	Protein: 3 gm	Fat Calories: 36
Total Fat: 4 gm	Dietary Fiber: 3 gm	Saturated Fat: 0.5 gm	Carbs: 6 gm
Sodium: 139 mg	Fat Component: 39%	Cholesterol: 0 mg	Calcium: 103 mg

Herbed Cauliflower

This enticing cream sauce can also be spooned over other vegetables.

1 clove minced garlic

½ teaspoon butter

1 head cauliflower

¼ cup dry white wine

½ cup skim milk

6 sundried tomatoes, diced

2 stalks celery with leaves

2 teaspoons chopped parsley

¼ teaspoon basil

¼ teaspoon rosemary

½ teaspoon pepper

½ cup grated lowfat
    Swiss Lorraine cheese

Serves 4

In a medium saucepan, sauté garlic in butter. Cut cauliflower into florets, and add to saucepan with wine, milk, sundried tomatoes and whole celery stalks. Cover, and slowly simmer 10 minutes. Remove cauliflower with slotted spoon, then add remaining spices to broth. Cook down until liquid is consistency of light cream. Remove celery stalks. Whisk in grated cheese until smooth. Add cauliflower to warm for 4 minutes.

Serving: 1/4 recipe	Calories: 104	Protein: 10 gm	Fat Calories: 27
Total Fat: 3 gm	Dietary Fiber: 6 gm	Saturated Fat: 2 gm	Carbs: 10 gm
Sodium: 162 mg	Fat Component: 26%	Cholesterol: 10 mg	Calcium: 228 mg

Fresh Corn Season

The word "corn" is short for "Indian corn," but refers to what most of the world knows as maize. In 18th-century America, it was the main food staple of both settlers and Native Americans. The crop helped forge a bond between the two groups. Indian women taught the newcomers to start planting "when the oak leaf is as big as a mouse's ear," by poking a hole in the ground, dropping in 4 or 5 kernels, and a chunk of fish for fertilizer. Indigenous North Americans also added ashes to cornmeal. We now know that the alkali in ash releases the B-vitamin niacin in corn. The traditional historical legend predicting a good harvest if the corn was "knee-high by the Fourth of July" is now routinely exceeded by newer hybrids. Sweet corn on-the-cob comes in shades of yellow and white, is high in sugars and low in starch. Popcorn is a variant that actually explodes when heated.

Massachusetts corn and fields

Fresh Roasted Corn

Serves 1

2 ears freshly harvested
corn in the husk

½ tablespoon butter
for every 2 ears

1 teaspoon salt

Pull husks down just far enough to remove silk. Run water into ear, drain, close husk and twist shut. Roast ears over hot coals on grill, or in 400º oven for 20 minutes, turning occasionally. In a tall pot, warm water with butter and salt, then cool slightly for butter to float up. Pull back husk to dangle and dip ear in buttered water. Allow excess to drip into the pot, and a light film of butter will coat the corn.

Serving: 2 ears	Calories: 64	Protein: 1 gm	Fat Calories: 9
Total Fat: 1 gm	Dietary Fiber: 1 gm	Saturated Fat: 0 gm	Carbs: 10 gm
Sodium: 36 mg	Fat Component: 14%	Cholesterol: 1 mg	Calcium: 1 mg

Savory Succotash

Serves 8

2 cups cooked lima beans

2 cups cooked corn kernels

½ cup nonfat powdered milk

½ cup skim milk

½ teaspoon basil

½ teaspoon pepper

salt to taste

1 clove garlic, pressed

¼ cup finely diced onion

1 tablespoon butter

Heat lima beans by boiling in water for 5 minutes. Drain and return to pot with corn. Dissolve powdered milk in skim milk, stir milk and spices into pot.

In a small pan, sauté garlic and onion in butter. Add to pot. Simmer 20 minutes, but do not boil.

Serving: 1/6 recipe	Calories: 160	Protein: 9 gm	Fat Calories: 18
Total Fat: 2 gm	Dietary Fiber: 5 gm	Saturated Fat: 1 gm	Carbs: 28 gm
Sodium: 76 mg	Fat Component: 11%	Cholesterol: 6 mg	Calcium: 103 mg

Zucchini Hash Browns

August's annual Vermont Zucchini Festival is hosted by Ludlow, in Okemo Valley. The big event includes a zucchini bake-off, live music, zucchini carvings, zukapult, and Mr. and Mrs. Zucchini Head contests.

3 cups packed grated zucchini   *Serves 4*

1 cup packed grated potatoes

2 tablespoons flour

1 tablespoon grated onion

1 tablespoon chopped parsley

1 teaspoon pepper

pinch of salt

½ teaspoon garlic powder

2 egg whites, beaten

1 tablespoon canola oil

Lay paper towels over a cotton kitchen towel. Place grated zucchini and potatoes on towels, fold together, twist and wring. In a large bowl, combine zucchini and potatoes, toss with flour. Stir in onion, parsley and spices. Let mixture rest 15 minutes, then stir in egg whites and oil, just until combined. Warm a nonstick frying pan on medium-high heat. Fry hash browns in patties until crispy on both sides.

Serving: 1/4 recipe	Calories: 140	Protein: 5 gm	Fat Calories: 36
Total Fat: 4 gm	Dietary Fiber: 3 gm	Saturated Fat: 0.5 gm	Carbs: 18 gm
Sodium: 66 mg	Fat Component: 26%	Cholesterol: 0 mg	Calcium: 33 mg

Clockwise from top left: Vermont's Essex Mountains, hay field on Vermont side of Lake Champlain across from New York's Adirondacks, Lake Harvey, Vermont round barn, lawn overlooking Lake Champlain, West Arlington covered bridge, early evening on a Vermont farm.

Mushroom Quiche

A mixture of two fresh varieties will make a flavorful pie.
Try button, porcini, portobella, chanterelle and oyster mushrooms.

Pastry crust:

Serves 6

1 tablespoon canola oil

1 egg, beaten

1½ cups unbleached flour

2-3 tablespoons ice water

Filling:

¼ cup diced onion

1 teaspoon canola oil

2 cups sliced mushrooms

3 eggs

1 cup nonfat buttermilk

½ teaspoon pepper

pinch of salt

½ teaspoon paprika

2 tablespoons chopped parsley

1 cup lowfat shredded Cheddar cheese

In a mixing bowl, use a fork or pastry cutter to work oil and egg evenly through flour. Make a well in the center of the flour, and add just enough ice water so dough holds together in a ball. If it is sticky, add a little more flour. Wrap in plastic and refrigerate.

Sauté onion in oil until clear. Add mushrooms, and cook until liquid evaporates. Beat eggs with buttermilk. Stir in mushrooms, spices and ¾ cup cheese.

Roll out dough to fit a 9-inch pie plate. Fold down edges, crimp with fingers. Sprinkle ¼ cup cheese over bottom of shell. Stir and pour filling into shell. Bake 15 minutes at 375º. Lower heat to 325º, bake another 35 minutes or just until quiche is set.

Serving: 1/6 recipe	Calories: 191	Protein: 8 gm	Fat Calories: 72
Total Fat: 8 gm	Dietary Fiber: 0 gm	Saturated Fat: 1 gm	Carbs: 3 gm
Sodium: 207 mg	Fat Component: 38%	Cholesterol: 109 mg	Calcium: 38 mg

Roasted Asiago Peas

Roasting fresh vegetables brings out their flavor like nothing else.

2 cups fresh shelled peas

1 teaspoon olive oil

½ teaspoon pepper

¼ cup shredded Asiago or
Parmesan cheese

Serves 4

Simmer peas in slightly salted water for 8 minutes. Drain well, and pat dry on paper towels. In a small bowl, toss peas with oil, then spread on a nonstick baking pan, sprinkle with pepper and cheese. Place on rack about 8 inches from broiler. Watch closely, remove when cheese looks toasty.

Serving: 1/4 recipe	Calories: 213	Protein: 3 gm	Fat Calories: 23
Total Fat: 2.5 gm	Dietary Fiber: 5 gm	Saturated Fat: 1 gm	Carbs: 35 gm
Sodium: 101 mg	Fat Component: 11%	Cholesterol: 56 mg	Calcium: 187 mg

Two easy ways to roast vegetables:
1) Lightly precook, coat in a small
   amount of oil and briefly broil, or
2) Coat in a small amount of oil and
   slow-roast at 275° until tender.

Historic New England

Nathan Hale Homestead
Connecticut

Robert Frost Trail
Ripton, Vermont

Rosecliff Manor
Newport, Rhode Island

Old City Hall
Boston, Massachusetts

Shaker Homestead
New Hampshire

Fort Popham
Maine

Quick Stir-Fry Asparagus

Asparagus are part of the lily family, sending up new stalks spring through mid-summer. High in folic acid, potassium, fiber, vitamins B6, A, C and thiamin, they have no fat or cholesterol.

Serves 4

1 lb. fresh asparagus

1 teaspoon olive oil

¼ cup dry white wine

¼ teaspoon pepper

2 tablespoons grated
　　Romano cheese

Cut off dry base end of asparagus. If stalks are very thick, peel skin from lower end. Warm oil in pan over medium heat. Place asparagus in hot oil, keeping stalks parallel to maintain their good looks. Pour in white wine. Cover pan and steam 3 minutes. Uncover, toss lightly, and add wine if drying out. Asparagus are done when just barely tender. Place in serving dish, sprinkle with pepper and cheese.

Serving: 1/4 recipe	Calories: 71	Protein: 5 gm	Fat Calories: 27
Total Fat: 3 gm	Dietary Fiber: 1 gm	Saturated Fat: 1 gm	Carbs: 2 gm
Sodium: 65 mg	Fat Component: 38%	Cholesterol: 5 mg	Calcium: 68 mg

Artichoke Florentine

Artichoke Florentine is a popular Connecticut menu item. Some of the state's loveliest restaurants are hidden within country inns, or tucked away in romantic settings surrounded by woods and waterfalls.

8 fresh artichokes

1 lb. bag fresh spinach

1 tablespoon butter

1 tablespoon flour

¾ cup skim milk

1 egg yolk

¼ teaspoon nutmeg

¼ teaspoon white pepper

½ cup lowfat shredded
    white Cheddar cheese

Serves 4

Slice off stem of artichokes. To open artichokes, push leaves apart, turn upside down on counter and press firmly on bottom. Remove fuzzy choke with spoon. Boil in water 20 minutes. Pull off leaves (save for a nice snack) and heart will remain. Cut hearts into quarters, place in a small nonstick baking pan.

Wash spinach, discard stems. Steam just until wilted. Drain, chop and press out moisture. Melt butter in saucepan, blend in flour to make a roux. Whisk in milk, yolk, spices and cheese. Cook until thickened, stirring constantly, then fold in spinach. Spoon over artichoke hearts. Bake 10 minutes at 400º.

Serving: 1/6 recipe	Calories: 128	Protein: 6 gm	Fat Calories: 36
Total Fat: 4 gm	Dietary Fiber: 4 gm	Saturated Fat: 2 gm	Carbs: 10 gm
Sodium: 194 mg	Fat Component: 28%	Cholesterol: 43 mg	Calcium: 154 mg

Connecticut scenery: Hartford waterfalls,
lake and pond reflections, Long Island Sound.

Spinach Frittata

A frittata is an Italian-style omelette with the filling
mixed into the eggs. It can be served at any meal of the day.

½ teaspoon olive oil

2 cloves garlic, minced

4 sundried tomatoes

1 onion, diced

1 cup corn kernels

1 cup fresh spinach leaves

4 eggs

2 egg whites

½ teaspoon pepper

1 teaspoon dill

2 tablespoons shredded
   Cheddar cheese

1 teaspoon paprika

Serves 4

In a large saucepan over medium heat, sauté garlic, tomatoes, onion and corn in oil, until onion is clear. Add spinach, cook 1 minute more. Drain off liquid.

Preheat oven to 350º. In a large mixing bowl, whisk eggs, whites, pepper and dill. Stir in vegetables and cheese. Pour into oiled oven dish and sprinkle with paprika. Bake 20 minutes, or until eggs are set.

Serving: 1/4 recipe	Calories: 151	Protein: 12 gm	Fat Calories: 59
Total Fat: 6.5 gm	Dietary Fiber: 3 gm	Saturated Fat: 1.5 gm	Carbs: 15 gm
Sodium: 370 mg	Fat Component: 39%	Cholesterol: 164 mg	Calcium: 151 mg

Spicy Roasted Potatoes

Legend claims Londonderry, New Hampshire, as the first place in North America where potatoes were grown, having been brought by Scottish and Irish settlers in the mid-1700s.

16-20 small red potatoes

2 egg whites

1 teaspoon Dijon mustard

1 teaspoon vinegar

1 tablespoon paprika

¼ teaspoon cumin

¼ teaspoon garlic

¼ teaspoon salt

¼ teaspoon pepper

2 teaspoons olive oil

Serves 4

Scrub potatoes, halve, then cut into ½-inch-thick slices. Pierce each 3-4 times with fork. In a large bowl, whisk remaining ingredients. Toss in potatoes, let stand 15 minutes, stirring every few minutes.

Coat a nonstick oven pan with oil. Use a slotted spoon to spread potatoes on pan. Roast, turning occasionally, at 400° for 40 minutes or until golden.

Serving: 1/4 recipe	Calories: 104	Protein: 5 gm	Fat Calories: 9
Total Fat: 1 gm	Dietary Fiber: 3 gm	Saturated Fat: 0 gm	Carbs: 20 gm
Sodium: 91 mg	Fat Component: 9%	Cholesterol: 0 mg	Calcium: 30 mg

View of the world from 6,288' above sea level. The world-record wind-gust speed of 231 mph is held here at the top of Mt. Washington, New Hampshire. Not far away, though quite far below, is New Hampshire's Lake Winnepesaukee. The lake is summer home and nesting site for hundreds of loons and ducks.

Farmers' Markets

New England has almost 400 farmers' markets and just as many farm stands. Most areas in the country now boast of their quality farm markets; look in a local paper for one nearby. Markets are generally open spring until late fall, and a few have permanent heated structures. By mid-summer when the harvest is at peak, farm stands are overflowing with a bountiful variety of fresh fruits, flowers and vegetables. Farmers' markets not only have the freshest produce, but they also support small farming families, many who farm organically. Organic farms contribute to your health and the environment through beneficial agricultural practices. Local markets offer produce too delicate to ship, heirloom varieties, and the opportunity to talk to the source – the farmer who grew it.

Chilled Green Beans

While you're toasting, add a few cups of sunflower, sesame, almond slivers or chopped nuts. Freeze to preserve the freshness of their oils. Nuts and seeds are an important part of a healthy diet.

¼ cup sunflower seeds

1 lb. fresh green beans
  (2½ cups cut)

¼ cup chopped onion

1 clove minced garlic

1 tablespoon olive oil

2 tablespoons vinegar

1 teaspoon lemon juice

¼ cup diced pimientos

½ teaspoon pepper

salt to taste

Serves 6

Spread sunflower seeds in a dry baking pan and toast at 325º until lightly browned.

Snap off tips of beans. Pull off tough filament when removing tips of larger beans. Cut into 1"-2" lengths. Steam in covered pot until tender. Drain.

Combine remaining ingredients, except seeds, and pour over green beans. Toss and chill. Just before serving, sprinkle with toasted seeds.

Serving: 1/6 recipe	Calories: 60	Protein: 2 gm	Fat Calories: 27
Total Fat: 3 gm	Dietary Fiber: 3 gm	Saturated Fat: 1 gm	Carbs: 7 gm
Sodium: 67 mg	Fat Component: 45%	Cholesterol: 1 mg	Calcium: 62 mg

Rutabaga Mash

"Turnip pudding" is also called "neeps" in Scotland, and "colcannon" by the Irish. It is on the menu of the Annual Kinsale, Ireland Festival of Fine Food in Newport, Rhode Island.

2 lbs. rutabagas

1 tablespoon butter

1 cup nonfat plain yogurt, sour cream or buttermilk

salt and pepper to taste

Serves 6

Peel rutabagas. Dice into ½-inch cubes. Steam 20 minutes, or until tender. Drain. Transfer rutabagas into large bowl, stir in butter, dairy, salt and pepper. Mash together. Serve hot.

Serving: 1/6 recipe	Calories: 81	Protein: 3 gm	Fat Calories: 18
Total Fat: 2 gm	Dietary Fiber: 0 gm	Saturated Fat: 1 gm	Carbs: 13 gm
Sodium: 86 mg	Fat Component: 22%	Cholesterol: 6 mg	Calcium: 111 mg

Upper row: Six young swans with adult on Narragansett Bay,
Rhode Island farm, Newport Cliff Walk House, Inlet near Newport.
Lower row: Providence, Rhode Island shore, Port Judith Light, Block Island Regatta.

Rhode Island's Local Food Forum coordinates innovative programs with Brown University, farmers, private foundations and state departments to discuss local, sustainable agriculture and create a vibrant local food economy. Similar successful programs have also been started throughout the other New England states, and also across the country. These organizations provide resources for quality fresh produce and dairy, and assist farmers with organic environmental practices.

Onion Pie au Gratin

A passion for onions is not required to bring on rave reviews.

Serves 6

1 egg, separated

4 cups diced onion

2 teaspoons canola oil

3 eggs

1 cup skim milk

½ cup nonfat dry
   powdered milk

1 teaspoon Worcestershire
   sauce

¾ cup shredded Parmesan
   cheese

Lightly grease a 9-inch pie plate. Whisk egg white, then brush over the bottom and sides of pie plate.

Sauté onion in oil until nearly clear. In a mixing bowl, beat 3 eggs and remaining yolk, milks and Worcestershire sauce. Stir in grated cheese and sautéed onion. Pour into pie plate. Bake at 375º for 30 minutes, or until golden brown.

Serving: 1/6 recipe	Calories: 127	Protein: 9 gm	Fat Calories: 68
Total Fat: 7.5 gm	Dietary Fiber: 1 gm	Saturated Fat: 2 gm	Carbs: 9 gm
Sodium: 212 mg	Fat Component: 53%	Cholesterol: 114 mg	Calcium: 199 mg

Desserts

Strawberry Crisp.....................................149

Blackberry Clafouti..................................150

Plums in Sweet Vermouth Sauce.............151

Wild Blueberry Pie.................................152

Glazed Apple Kuchen..............................153

Peach Crumb Cobbler............................155

Boston Cream Pie..................................156

White Grape Sorbet...............................157

Portsmouth Pear Spice Cake....................158

Vermont's Finest Maple-Hazelnut Torte 160

Chocolate-Pecan Oatmeal Cookies.............161

A Summer's Night Chocolate Kisses...........162

Apple Indian Pudding.............................163

Raspberry Pie......................................165

Lemon Cheesecake with Blueberry Topping...166

Chocolate Needham Squares.....................167

Strawberry Crisp

You already know the favored topping for this crisp!

Serves 8

4 cups strawberries,
   hulled and halved

2 tablespoons cornstarch

½ cup sugar

1 tablespoon lemon juice

½ cup unbleached flour

1 cup rolled oats

½ cup packed brown sugar

½ teaspoon cinnamon

pinch of salt

2 tablespoons butter,
   melted

1 egg, beaten

Preheat oven to 350º. Grease a 9-inch square baking dish. Toss strawberries with cornstarch, sugar and lemon juice. Place in baking dish.

Mix flour, oats, brown sugar, cinnamon and salt. Sprinkle with butter, then use fork to mix evenly. Stir in egg, then distribute over strawberries. Bake 25 minutes, or until golden browned.

Serving: 1/8 recipe	Calories: 229	Protein: 3 gm	Fat Calories: 36
Total Fat: 4 gm	Dietary Fiber: 2 gm	Saturated Fat: 2 gm	Carbs: 45 gm
Sodium: 59 mg	Fat Component: 16%	Cholesterol: 35 mg	Calcium: 32 mg

Blackberry Clafouti

Blackberries grow wild all over New England. The wooded shoreline has so many that local berry lovers can't eat them all!

2 cups fresh blackberries

¾ cup nonfat plain yogurt

¾ cup nonfat cottage cheese

½ cup skim milk

1 egg

½ teaspoon vanilla

¼ cup unbleached flour

½ cup sugar

pinch of cinnamon

Serves 4

Boil a kettle of water, and preheat oven to 425º. Lightly butter 4 custard cups. Spread blackberries in bottom of cups. In a blender, process remaining ingredients until completely smooth. Pour mixture over berries. Set cups into a deep baking dish, and fill with boiling water to about half the depth of the cups. Bake 25 minutes, or just until custard is set.

Clafouti can be served warm or cold in the custard cups. When chilled, you can run a knife around the edges and invert onto dessert plates.

Serving: 1/4 recipe	Calories: 218	Protein: 11 gm	Fat Calories: 18
Total Fat: 2 gm	Dietary Fiber: 4 gm	Saturated Fat: 0 gm	Carbs: 41 gm
Sodium: 223 mg	Fat Component: 8%	Cholesterol: 55 mg	Calcium: 160 mg

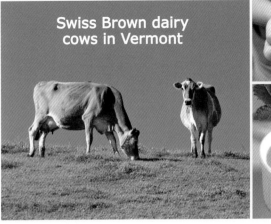

Swiss Brown dairy cows in Vermont

Plums in Sweet Vermouth Sauce

Keep a bottle of inexpensive vermouth available for cooking.
It is just as flavorful as "cooking vermouth" and half the price.

2 lbs. fresh plums

½ cup packed brown sugar

½ cup vermouth

pinch of salt

¼ cup water

Serves 4

Concassé plums: Boil a large pot of water. With a paring knife, score an "X" in top and bottom of plums. Boil for 5 minutes, then remove with slotted spoon. When cool, the skins will peel off easily.

Cut plums into large bite-size pieces. Combine in saucepan with brown sugar, vermouth, salt and water. Cook over medium-high heat, stirring occasionally, about 25 minutes, until plums are tender and sauce thickens. If needed, add more water.

Serving: 1/2 cup	Calories: 172	Protein: 2 gm	Fat Calories: 9
Total Fat: 1 gm	Dietary Fiber: 2 gm	Saturated Fat: 0 gm	Carbs: 38 gm
Sodium: 28 mg	Fat Component: 5%	Cholesterol: 0 mg	Calcium: 23 mg

Wild Blueberry Pie

Homemade blueberry pie! One of the simple things that make life sweet.

Crust:

2½ cups unbleached flour

3 tablespoons sugar

6 tablespoons canola oil

6 tablespoons ice water

1 tablespoon skim milk

Blueberry Filling:

4 cups blueberries, fresh
   wild berries if available

½ cup sugar

¼ cup brown sugar

1 tablespoon quick tapioca

½ teaspoon cinnamon

½ teaspoon nutmeg

1 tablespoon lemon juice

1 tablespoon skim milk

Makes 9-inch pie

Preheat oven to 400º. Grease a 9-inch pie plate.

Mix flour and sugar. Use a fork to distribute oil through flour mixture, then blend in water and milk. Divide dough in half, and roll each between sheets of wax paper. Place bottom crust in pie plate.

Clean blueberries and put into bowl (if canned or frozen drain first in sieve). In a separate bowl, mix sugars, tapioca, cinnamon and nutmeg. Sprinkle lemon juice on blueberries, then gently fold into sugar mixture. Let rest 45 minutes, stir and pour into shell. For the top: use a rolling lattice cutter, make strips to weave, or place solid dough on pie and make 5 slits to vent. Seal edges with milk, flute with fork. Bake 10 minutes at 400º, then reduce to 350º to bake 35 minutes more. Cool before serving.

Serving: 1 piece	Calories: 371	Protein: 5 gm	Fat Calories: 99
Total Fat: 11 gm	Dietary Fiber: 3 gm	Saturated Fat: 1 gm	Carbs: 65 gm
Sodium: 11 mg	Fat Component: 27%	Cholesterol: 0 mg	Calcium: 25 mg

Glazed Apple Kuchen

Not so difficult, but oh so pretty!

Serves 8

Crust:

1¼ cups flour

¼ cup sugar

1 teaspoon baking powder

¼ cup canola oil

2 eggs

1 tablespoon melted butter

Fruit and Glaze:

1 cup apple juice

1 teaspoon lemon juice

2 tablespoons sugar

3 cups peeled apple slices, ¾"-thick at outer edge

1 teaspoon almond extract

Finish:

¼ cup powdered sugar

Grease a 10-inch fluted springform pan. Combine flour, sugar and baking powder. Use a fork to evenly distributed oil, then mix in eggs. Dab dough over bottom of pan; freeze 15 minutes. Flour fingertips, press dough over bottom and 1 inch up sides of pan. Bake 15 minutes at 350º. Cool. Brush with butter.

Simmer juices and sugar. Poach half of the apples for 5 minutes, remove with a slotted spoon and drain in sieve. Repeat process with remaining apples. Boil down syrup until ¼ cup remains. Stir in extract and remove from heat. Arrange apples in shell and drizzle with syrup. Bake 15 minutes at 350º. Cool, remove from pan, and sift powdered sugar on top.

Serving: 1/8 recipe	Calories: 210	Protein: 5 gm	Fat Calories: 72
Total Fat: 8 gm	Dietary Fiber: 2 gm	Saturated Fat: 1 gm	Carbs: 24 gm
Sodium: 151 mg	Fat Component: 34%	Cholesterol: 54 mg	Calcium: 115 mg

Peaches

Peaches are succulent and firm, with sweet nectar unlike any other fruit. Choose fruit that smells sweet, yields to gentle pressure, and is not mushy. A peach without fuzz is a nectarine, which should be a bit firmer. They are interchangeable in cooking, but nectarines don't need peeling. Easily peel peaches by poaching in boiling water 1 minute, then plunge into ice water. When cool, slice into the skin and pull it off. The pit of freestone varieties separates from the flesh. To pit clingstones, slice wedges from flower end to stem end, then pull apart. Sprinkle with lemon juice to prevent darkening. Hardy peach trees for New England are Elberta, Reliance, Cresthaven, Redhaven and Red Globe; nectarines are Sunglo, Red Gold and Arctic Glo.

Peach Crumb Cobbler

A perfect match with vanilla frozen yogurt or ice cream.

Filling: *Serves 8*

6 cups peeled peach slices

½ cup sugar

1 teaspoon cinnamon

1 tablespoon cornstarch

2 tablespoons white wine

2 teaspoons lemon juice

Topping:

1 cup unbleached flour

½ cup packed brown sugar

2 teaspoons cinnamon

2 tablespoons butter,
   softened

Preheat oven to 350º. Grease a 9" x 12" deep-dish baking pan. In a mixing bowl, combine peaches, sugar, cinnamon and cornstarch, toss to coat. Mix in wine and lemon juice. Pour into prepared pan.

Combine flour with brown sugar and cinnamon. Use a fork to distribute butter until mixture resembles coarse crumbs. Sprinkle over peaches. Bake 45 minutes. Serve hot or cold.

Serving: 1/8 recipe	Calories: 212	Protein: 2 gm	Fat Calories: 27
Total Fat: 3 gm	Dietary Fiber: 3 gm	Saturated Fat: 2 gm	Carbs: 46 gm
Sodium: 36 mg	Fat Component: 13%	Cholesterol: 8 mg	Calcium: 27 mg

*This filling also makes the Peach Pie on the front cover.
Use crust and baking directions on page 152.*

Boston Cream Pie

Actually a layer cake adapted from the early American "Pudding-cake Pie." In 1996, Boston Cream Pie was named the official Massachusetts State Dessert.

Makes 9-inch round cake

Cake Batter:

4 tablespoons unsalted butter, softened

2½ cups sifted cake flour

1 tablespoon baking powder

½ teaspoon salt

1¾ cups sugar

1 cup skim milk

1 teaspoon vanilla

3 eggs

Cream Filling:

½ cup sugar

1½ tablespoons cornstarch

1½ cups skim milk

1 egg yolk, beaten

1 teaspoon vanilla

Fudge Glaze:

½ cup sugar

½ cup unsweetened cocoa powder

¾ cup nonfat buttermilk

½ teaspoon vanilla

Preheat oven to 350°. Grease and flour two 9-inch round cake pans. In a large bowl, use electric beaters to whip batter ingredients for 3 minutes. Pour into pans. Bake 30 minutes, or until toothpick inserted in cakes comes out clean. Cool cakes on wire rack.

In a saucepan, whisk cream filling sugar, cornstarch, milk and egg over medium heat until mixture boils for 1 minute. Remove from heat, add vanilla. Chill.

In a saucepan over medium heat, whisk together fudge glaze ingredients, except vanilla. Stir constantly until mixture boils for 2 minutes. Remove from heat, add vanilla. Cool to room temperature.

When everything is cool, spread cream on top of one cake, set second cake on top. Spread glaze on top.

Serving: 1 piece	Calories: 499	Protein: 10 gm	Fat Calories: 81
Total Fat: 9 gm	Dietary Fiber: 2 gm	Saturated Fat: 5 gm	Carbs: 95 gm
Sodium: 379 mg	Fat Component: 16%	Cholesterol: 98 mg	Calcium: 181 mg

Boston Gardens

White Grape Sorbet

Just right between formal dinner courses, or for a light finish.

1 lb. white seedless grapes
½ cup apple juice
¼ cup sugar

Serves 4

Process grapes in blender. Strain liquid into saucepan. Add apple juice and sugar. Stir over low heat until sugar is dissolved.

Pour into an 8-inch square pan and set in freezer. Use a rubber spatula to stir every 15 minutes until mixture is creamy, about 2 hours. Cover and allow to freeze. To serve, scoop into small dishes, garnish with mint, if desired.

Serving: 1/4 recipe	Calories: 135	Protein: 1 gm	Fat Calories: 5
Total Fat: 0.5 gm	Dietary Fiber: 1 gm	Saturated Fat: 0 gm	Carbs: 36 gm
Sodium: 3 mg	Fat Component: 3%	Cholesterol: 0 mg	Calcium: 18 mg

Portsmouth Pear Spice Cake

Hardy pear varieties grow throughout New England.
This cake is moist and marvelous!

Batter:

Serves 10

1½ cups packed brown
    sugar

½ cup butter, softened

1 cup applesauce

1 teaspoon vanilla

1 tablespoon baking powder

½ teaspoon baking soda

2 teaspoons cinnamon

½ teaspoon ground ginger

½ teaspoon ground cloves

2½ cups sifted cake flour

3 eggs

3 medium-size ripe pears

Frosting:

3 tablespoons skim milk

16 oz. nonfat cream cheese

1 teaspoon vanilla

2½ cups powdered sugar

1 cup chopped pecans

½ cup fresh berries

Preheat oven to 350º. Grease and flour round springform cake pan. With electric beaters, blend sugar, butter, applesauce, vanilla, baking powder, baking soda, cinnamon, ginger, cloves and flour on medium-high speed 5 minutes, then beat in eggs.

Peel and chop pears into very small pieces. With a rubber spatula, fold into batter, then spread in pan. Bake 45 minutes, or until toothpick inserted in cake comes out clean. Remove from pan. Cool on rack before frosting.

Frosting: Combine milk, cream cheese and vanilla with electric beater until fluffy. Slowly sift in powdered sugar until frosting is desired consistency. Spread and decorate cake with frosting. Press pecans into sides of cake, arrange berries on top.

Serving: 1 piece	Calories: 353	Protein: 8 gm	Fat Calories: 72
Total Fat: 8 gm	Dietary Fiber: 3 gm	Saturated Fat: 3 gm	Carbs: 65 gm
Sodium: 226 mg	Fat Component: 20%	Cholesterol: 65 mg	Calcium: 133 mg

North Woods' Neighbors

Black Bear

Moose

White-tailed Deer

The Northern Forest Eco-Region spans sections of New Hampshire, Maine, Vermont and New York. The 26 million acres are now the largest forest system in the east. Selecting products made from sustainable well-managed forests (like the woodpulp for this book's paper) helps preserve the habitat and lives of woodland creatures.

Elk

Bobcat

Vermont's Finest Maple-Hazelnut Torte

Serves 10

Batter:

6 eggs, separated

1 cup sugar

½ cup bread crumbs, (coarse, not fine)

¼ cup unsweetened grated chocolate

½ cup coarsely ground hazelnuts

2 tablespoons maple syrup

1 teaspoon vanilla

½ teaspoon baking powder

½ teaspoon cinnamon

Maple Sugar Icing:

2 cups powdered sugar

1 tablespoon skim milk

½ teaspoon vanilla

¼ cup maple syrup (more or less)

Hazelnuts, filberts and cobnuts are all the same nut.

Preheat oven to 325º. Have all ingredients at room temperature. Beat egg yolks until light and lemon-colored. Sift sugar, then slowly beat it into the yolks. Add all other ingredients except egg whites.

In separate bowl, beat egg whites until stiff. Gently fold into batter. Pour batter into lightly greased and floured 9-inch springform pan. Bake 1 hour. Remove from pan. Cool on wire rack before icing.

Icing: Sift powdered sugar. Blend in milk and vanilla. Stir in maple syrup to desired consistency (thick if spreading on cake, thinner if pouring over pieces).

Serving: 1 piece	Calories: 303	Protein: 5 gm	Fat Calories: 81
Total Fat: 9 gm	Dietary Fiber: 1 gm	Saturated Fat: 2 gm	Carbs: 61 gm
Sodium: 128 mg	Fat Component: 27%	Cholesterol: 129 mg	Calcium: 72 mg

Chocolate-Pecan Oatmeal Cookies

(Although reduced in fat, eating cookies by the dozen does
not follow the guidelines of the American Heart Association!)

Makes 48 cookies

4 tablespoons butter,
   softened

½ cup packed brown sugar

½ cup granulated sugar

1 egg

1 teaspoon vanilla

¼ cup apple juice
   concentrate

1 cup unbleached flour

½ teaspoon baking soda

½ teaspoon baking powder

1 cup uncooked quick
   rolled oats

½ cup mini chocolate chips

¼ cup chopped pecans

Preheat oven to 350º. Grease cookie sheet. Cream together butter and sugars. Beat in egg, vanilla and apple juice concentrate.

In a separate bowl, sift together flour, baking soda and baking powder. Beat into liquid mixture. When smooth, mix in rolled oats, then chocolate chips and nuts. Drop batter by heaping teaspoons, 2 inches apart, on cookie sheet. Bake 10-12 minutes or until cookie bottoms are light brown.

Serving: 1 cookie	Calories: 45	Protein: 1 gm	Fat Calories: 14
Total Fat: 1.5 gm	Dietary Fiber: 0 gm	Saturated Fat: 0.5 gm	Carbs: 6 gm
Sodium: 27 mg	Fat Component: 30%	Cholesterol: 9 mg	Calcium: 7 mg

An afternoon stroll with treats beneath the crab apple trees. Aren't you grateful to know what makes a proper snack?

A Summer's Night Chocolate Kisses

Like all sweet kisses, these too will disappear too soon!

6 egg whites

pinch of salt

½ teaspoon cream of tartar

¼ cup granulated sugar

½ cup powdered sugar

3 tablespoons cocoa
　　powder

Makes 36 meringues

Beat egg whites with salt and cream of tartar until foamy. Slowly beat in granulated sugar, 1 tablespoon at a time (the meringue should become stiff). Sift powdered sugar and cocoa over meringue, and use spatula to gently fold into meringue.

Transfer to pastry bag or icing dispenser with large star-shaped nozzle. Form into large kisses on greased nonstick baking sheet. Bake 25-30 minutes at 200°, just until outsides are firm to the touch. These kisses are very fragile, so handle with TLC!

Serving: 1 kiss	Calories: 20	Protein: 1 gm	Fat Calories: 5
Total Fat: 0.5 gm	Dietary Fiber: 0 gm	Saturated Fat: 0 gm	Carbs: 4 gm
Sodium: 10 mg	Fat Component: 23%	Cholesterol: 0 mg	Calcium: 1 mg

Apple Indian Pudding

A New England tradition. Serve hot with lowfat whipped or ice cream.

Serves 6

2½ cups skim milk

½ cup yellow cornmeal

pinch of salt

½ cup molasses

½ cup sugar

2 teaspoons cinnamon

1 egg

2 cups peeled and finely
    diced apples

Scald 2 cups milk over medium-high heat. Stir while slowly adding cornmeal, salt, molasses, sugar and cinnamon. Remove from heat. Beat egg, and whisk into pudding. Stir in apples. Pour into 2-quart greased baking dish, cover. Bake at 325° for 1 hour. Remove from oven. Without stirring, pour remaining ½ cup milk over pudding. Bake uncovered until milk is absorbed, about 1½-2 hours.

Serving: 1/6 recipe	Calories: 225	Protein: 5 gm	Fat Calories: 9
Total Fat: 1 gm	Dietary Fiber: 2 gm	Saturated Fat: 0.5 gm	Carbs: 50 gm
Sodium: 89 mg	Fat Component: 4%	Cholesterol: 38 mg	Calcium: 242 mg

Pies and Tarts

Pies are the quintessential American dessert – topped with crumbs, lattice, crusts, meringue, cream, glaze or open faced – pie makes us feel at home. Pastry dough is simply flour, fat, liquid, and maybe salt or sugar. Dough made from unbleached or white whole wheat flour is easier to work, and healthier too. Flaky pie crusts are defined by a lower ratio of fat than tart shells. Tarts are topless, with straighter sides, and a more buttery pastry to produce a stiffer, crumbly shell. Heat is the enemy of delicate crusts, so use a pastry cutter to cut fat into the flour. Chill dough an hour before rolling out pie crust, or pressing tart pastry into pan.

Raspberry Pie

Raspberry plants are good multipliers. Allow space for raspberry patch expansion, and you'll have enough raspberries for many summer pies!

Crust:

Makes 9-inch pie

2½ cups unbleached flour

3 tablespoons sugar

¼ cup canola oil

6 tablespoons ice water

1 tablespoon skim milk

1 teaspoon melted butter

Raspberry Filling:

4 cups fresh raspberries

1 teaspoon vanilla

¾ cup sugar

2 tablespoons cornstarch

2 tablespoons orange juice

Grease and flour a 9-inch pie plate. Combine flour and sugar. With pastry cutter or knives, cut oil into mixture. Blend in water and milk. Divide dough in half and roll each between sheets of wax paper. Place bottom crust in pie plate; do not trim edges. Brush shell with melted butter.

Sprinkle raspberries with vanilla and sugar. Whisk cornstarch into orange juice, then stir into raspberries. Let mixture rest 30 minutes, then transfer to pie shell. Use lattice roller to prepare top crust, or slice remaining dough into strips and weave over top. Use a little milk to seal strips to pie shell. Trim edge. Bake 40 minutes at 350º.

Serving: 1 piece	Calories: 345	Protein: 5 gm	Fat Calories: 72
Total Fat: 8 gm	Dietary Fiber: 5 gm	Saturated Fat: 1 gm	Carbs: 63 gm
Sodium: 4 mg	Fat Component: 21%	Cholesterol: 0 mg	Calcium: 25 mg

Lemon Cheesecake with Blueberry Topping

Serves 12

Cheesecake Crust:

2 cups sugared graham cracker crumbs

2 tablespoons canola oil

1 tablespoon lemon juice

Cheesecake Filling:

3 eggs

16 oz. light cream cheese, softened

16 oz. nonfat sour cream

½ cup part-skim ricotta cheese, well drained

2 tablespoons cornstarch

1½ cups sugar

2 tablespoons lemon juice

1 teaspoon finely grated lemon rind

2 teaspoons vanilla

pinch of salt

Blueberry Topping:

1½ cups blueberries

1 tablespoon quick tapioca

1 teaspoon lemon juice

½ cup sugar

Preheat oven to 375°. Combine crust ingredients in mixing bowl. Lightly grease a 9-inch springform pan. Press crust mixture into bottom of pan and 2½ inches up the sides. Bake 3 minutes, then chill.

Reduce oven to 325°. In blender, whip cheesecake ingredients until smooth. Pour into crust. Bake until only the center is not yet set, about 50 minutes. Turn oven off, leaving cheesecake inside for 1 hour. Cool at room temperature, then chill at least 6 hours.

Combine blueberries and tapioca in a saucepan, crushing a few berries to release juice. Cook over medium heat 5 minutes. Add lemon juice and sugar, simmer until thickened, about 15 minutes. Cool before spooning over cheesecake slices.

Serving: 1 piece	Calories: 345	Protein: 10 gm	Fat Calories: 99
Total Fat: 11 gm	Dietary Fiber: 1 gm	Saturated Fat: 5.5 gm	Carbs: 50 gm
Sodium: 358 mg	Fat Component: 29%	Cholesterol: 75 mg	Calcium: 128 mg

Chocolate Needham Squares

Nineteenth century trading ships returned from the Caribbean with sugar, molasses and coconuts, too. Finding a way to share the taste of coconut, Needhams were created by a Portland, Maine candy maker in 1872.

Makes 36 squares

1 cup cold mashed
   potatoes

1 cup powdered sugar

1½ cups shredded coconut

1 teaspoon vanilla

¼ teaspoon salt

4 squares semisweet
   baking chocolate

Whip together mashed potatoes, sugar, shredded coconut, vanilla and salt. Blend well and press into an 8-inch square pan.

Boil water in bottom pan of double boiler. In the top pan, melt chocolate. Pour melted chocolate over Needham mixture. When chocolate begins to cool, mark into 1¼-inch squares Repeat marking through cooling process and Needhams will not fracture when divided. Cool at room temperature.

Serving: 1 square	Calories: 67	Protein: 0 gm	Fat Calories: 18
Total Fat: 2 gm	Dietary Fiber: 1 gm	Saturated Fat: 1.5 gm	Carbs: 6 gm
Sodium: 18 mg	Fat Component: 27%	Cholesterol: 0 mg	Calcium: 5 mg

Seasonal Preserves and Jams

Cheery Cherry Jam....................................170
Machias' Best Blueberry Jam.........................171
Plum Jelly..172
Brandied Peach Preserves..........................173
Fresh Lemonade Syrup............................175
Tomato Preserves...................................176
Sweet Pepper Marmalade.........................177
Pickled Beets...178
Curried Apricot Chutney...........................179

Canning Procedures

Home canning is a process of preserving food within a closed jar by restricting the growth of unwanted microorganisms. This is accomplished by strict application of "heat processing" procedures that prevent food from spoiling at its normal rate.

Follow jar manufacturer's directions, not the Canning Procedures below, if:

You are using a recipe that is not in this book, or

your altitude is 1,000-feet or more above sea level, or

any procedures below conflict with jar manufacturer's directions.

1. Read through directions, assemble equipment, and boil water as needed.

2. Use only canning jars with new fitted rubber-rimmed airtight lids and metal screw-down bands. Discard jars, lids and bands with defects (e.g., chips, dents).

3. Sterilize jars in boiling water or dishwasher; keep hot until ready to fill. Sterilize lids and bands in a saucepan by slowly simmering, but do not boil.

4. Fill hot jars with hot filling, leaving space for recipe's headroom. Remove air bubbles by sliding a rubber spatula between filling and jar, press down on filling, and then run spatula around jar again. If needed, add filling to correct headroom.

5. Wipe rim and threads of jar clean with a damp cloth. Center lid on jar with rubber seal facing down. Screw on metal band, but no tighter than you can do with your fingertips. The lid must vent air to form a vacuum seal.

6. If using a deep steaming pot, place jars in empty pot so they don't touch. If using a canner and rack, use manufacturer's directions to set jars in canner.

7. Add boiling water to 1 inch above jars. Turn heat to high. Start counting the recipe's processing time when water boils. When processed, turn off heat, and remove steamer or canner lid. When safely cool, lift jars (not by the lid) without tilting, to cool on a towel. Do not handle for 24 hours.

8. After 24 hours, press down on the center of the lid. If a good seal has formed, the lid will not flex. Remove metal bands, and gently try lifting the lid. If the seal is airtight, the lid will not easily lift off. Refrigerate any poorly sealed jars.

9. Jars with airtight seals: Do not replace the bands. Wipe jars and lids clean with a damp cloth. Label with recipe name and date, and store in a cool, dark, dry place. Use within one year. Reconfirm a tight seal and fresh smell when opening.

Cheery Cherry Jam

The cherry flavor is wonderfully highlighted by the citrus accents.

3 lbs. ripe cherries
　(about 9 cups)

¼ cup water

1 cup orange juice

1 tablespoon lemon juice

2 cups sugar

See Canning Procedures, page 169.　　*Makes 4 pints*

Seed and quarter cherries. Simmer with water and juices 20 minutes. Stir in sugar until dissolved. Taste, add sugar or lemon juice as desired. Continue stirring and simmer 30 minutes more. Pour into hot sterilized jars by following directions on page 169, and allowing:

Headroom: ¼ inch
Processing time: 10 minutes

Serving: 2 tablespoons	Calories: 48	Protein: 0 gm	Fat Calories: 0
Total Fat: 0 gm	Dietary Fiber: 1 gm	Saturated Fat: 0 gm	Carbs: 13 gm
Sodium: 0 mg	Fat Component: 0%	Cholesterol: 0 mg	Calcium: 4 mg

Machias' Best Blueberry Jam

Machias, Maine is the heart of wild blueberry land. Stock up in late summer, they can be frozen whole; the season is short, but very sweet. As for the recipe, all blueberries will be pleased to be included in this jam!

2 quarts (8 cups)
   fresh blueberries

2 tablespoons lemon juice

1 package (1¾ oz.)
   powdered fruit pectin

6 cups sugar

See Canning Procedures, page 169.   Makes 4 pints

Clean stems and twigs from blueberries. In a large saucepan, crush 2 cups of blueberries. Mix in remaining blueberries, lemon juice and pectin. Place over high heat, stirring until mixture boils. Gently simmer just 1 minute and then add sugar. Stirring constantly, bring to a rolling boil 1 minute. Remove from heat, skim off foam. Ladle into sterilized jars, following directions on page 169, and allowing:

Headroom: ¼ inch
Processing time: 10 minutes

Serving: 2 tablespoons	Calories: 86	Protein: 0 gm	Fat Calories: 0
Total Fat: 0 gm	Dietary Fiber: 1 gm	Saturated Fat: 0 gm	Carbs: 13 gm
Sodium: 0 mg	Fat Component: 0%	Cholesterol: 0 mg	Calcium: 4 mg

This beautiful highbush blueberry is on a Vermont farm. Highbush varieties are bigger than their wild cousins. All blueberries are interchangeable in cooking.

Lowbush blueberries are ground cover plants, famously known as wild Maine blueberries. They only grow in glacial soil conditions unique to the region.

Plum Jelly

Look for Damson plums; they have an incredible plummy flavor.

4 lbs. very ripe plums
   (24 plums)

3 cups water

3 cups sugar

1 package (1¾ oz.)
   powdered fruit pectin

See Canning Procedures, page 169.   *Makes 4 pints*

Pit and quarter plums. Boil in water 40 minutes, then skim off froth.   Press pulp through large-meshed sieve.   Mix pulp with sugar and pectin, dissolve well. Return to pot and boil for 3 minutes, skimming froth.   Pour into hot sterilized jelly jars by following directions on page 169, and allowing:

Headroom: ¼ inch
Processing time: 10 minutes

Serving: 2 tablespoons	Calories: 59	Protein: 0 gm	Fat Calories: 0
Total Fat: 0 gm	Dietary Fiber: 0 gm	Saturated Fat: 0 gm	Carbs: 15 gm
Sodium: 0 mg	Fat Component: 0%	Cholesterol: 0 mg	Calcium: 1 mg

Brandied Peach Preserves

A light dessert or elegant accompaniment to a luncheon.

4 lbs. peaches, ripe but firm (16 peaches)

2 cups sugar

3 cups water

½ cup brandy

See Canning Procedures, page 169.   Makes 4 pints

Rub fuzz off peaches with a coarse towel. Rinse, pit and slice peaches. In a large pot, boil sugar and water, cook down into a syrup. Add peaches, and simmer 10 minutes. Use a slotted spoon to transfer into sterilized jars. Pour 2 tablespoons brandy over peaches in each jar, then fill with hot syrup by following directions on page 169, and allowing:

Headroom: ½ inch
Processing time: 15 minutes

Serving: 1/2 cup	Calories: 163	Protein: 1 gm	Fat Calories: 0
Total Fat: 0 gm	Dietary Fiber: 2 gm	Saturated Fat: 0 gm	Carbs: 38 gm
Sodium: 2 mg	Fat Component: 0%	Cholesterol: 0 mg	Calcium: 7 mg

Stonington Light
Connecticut

Lake Champlain
Vermont

Nauset Light, Cape Cod
Massachusetts

*New
England
Lighthouses*

Beavertail Lighthouse
Rhode Island

Portsmouth Harbor Light
New Hampshire

Portland Head Light
Maine

Fresh Lemonade Syrup

Serve syrup with tall glasses of ice water for customized lemonade.

2 cups sugar

1 cup water

rind of 2 lemons,
    cut into thin strips

juice of 6 squeezed lemons

Makes 2½ cups syrup

Boil sugar, water and rind for 10 minutes. Cool to room temperature and add freshly squeezed lemon juice. Strain the syrup and store in a glass jar. Chill. Syrup will keep at least 3 weeks in the refrigerator.

Lemonade: Chill glasses and fill with ice. Set out lemonade syrup and a pitcher of cold water. Place glasses on small doilies with tall stirring spoons and straws to complete setting for a summer cooler.

Serving: 4 tablespoons	Calories: 163	Protein: 0 gm	Fat Calories: 0
Total Fat: 0 gm	Dietary Fiber: 0 gm	Saturated Fat: 0 gm	Carbs: 43 gm
Sodium: 2 mg	Fat Component: 0%	Cholesterol: 0 mg	Calcium: 6 mg

Tomato Preserves

A tomato side dish or garnish that's surprisingly different.

2 lbs. ripe tomatoes

¼ cup sugar

1 lemon, thinly sliced and
   seeded

1 tablespoon grated fresh
   ginger, or 1 teaspoon
   ground ginger

See Canning Procedures, page 169.   Makes 2 pints

Scald and skin tomatoes. Place in bowl, mix with sugar and refrigerate 12 hours. Drain juice and boil down until thickened. Add lemon and ginger. Simmer for 20 minutes. Pack in hot sterilized jars by following directions on page 169, and allowing:

Headroom: ½ inch
Processing time: 10 minutes

Serving: 1/2 cup	Calories: 76	Protein: 1 gm	Fat Calories: 0
Total Fat: 0 gm	Dietary Fiber: 1 gm	Saturated Fat: 0 gm	Carbs: 19 gm
Sodium: 11 mg	Fat Component: 0%	Cholesterol: 0 mg	Calcium: 14 mg

Sweet Pepper Marmalade

A sweet-and-spicy accent for cheese, crackers and smoked meats.

12 red bell peppers

5 cloves garlic, minced

¼ cup olive oil

1 tablespoon ground ginger

½ cup orange juice

1 tablespoon lemon juice

3 tablespoons sugar

1 tablespoon brown sugar

1 teaspoon pepper

See Canning Procedures, page 169.   Makes 3 pints

Clean, seed and dice peppers into small pieces, about ¼ inch square. In a large pan, sauté garlic in oil over medium-low heat 5 minutes. Add peppers, stir, cover and simmer 10 minutes. Mix in remaining ingredients, cover and cook 25 minutes. Remove cover, stir frequently on low heat for 1 hour. Pack in hot sterilized jars by following directions on page 169, and allowing:

Headroom: ¼ inch
Processing time: 10 minutes

Serving: 2 tablespoons	Calories: 27	Protein: 0 gm	Fat Calories: 5
Total Fat: 0.5 gm	Dietary Fiber: 1 gm	Saturated Fat: 0 gm	Carbs: 3 gm
Sodium: 1 mg	Fat Component: 17%	Cholesterol: 0 mg	Calcium: 5 mg

Pickled Beets

Even better with baby beets, which don't need peeling.

2 lbs. beets

2 quarts water

2 tablespoons pickling salt

1½ cups vinegar

1½ cups water

1 cup sugar

1 teaspoon peppercorns

1 teaspoon mustard seed

See Canning Procedures, page 169.   Makes 4 pints

Boil beets 20 minutes in 2 quarts water with pickling salt. Drain, peel, slice or dice to desired size. Pack in sterilized jars. Boil all other ingredients together, and simmer for 3 minutes. Pour hot liquid over beets by following directions on page 169, and allowing:

Headroom: ½ inch
Processing time: 15 minutes

Serving: 1 cup	Calories: 154	Protein: 2 gm	Fat Calories: 3
Total Fat: 0.5 gm	Dietary Fiber: 4 gm	Saturated Fat: 0 gm	Carbs: 39 gm
Sodium: 99 mg	Fat Component: 2%	Cholesterol: 0 mg	Calcium: 24 mg

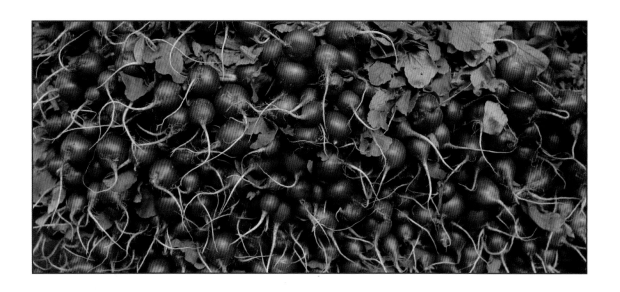

Curried Apricot Chutney

Chutney is a relish or condiment used to complement meat, fish or rice.

2 cups water

2 cups chopped dried
   apricots

½ cup finely chopped onion

½ cup sugar

1½ cups cider vinegar

1 teaspoon ground ginger

2 teaspoons curry powder

1 teaspoon cinnamon

pinch of salt

1 cup golden raisins

See Canning Procedures, page 169.   Makes 2 pints

Simmer water, apricots, onions and sugar together for 30 minutes. In a separate pot, cook vinegar and spices over medium heat 5 minutes. Combine mixtures and add raisins. Pack in hot sterilized jars by following directions on page 169, and allowing:

Headroom: ¼ inch
Processing time: 15 minutes

Serving: 2 tablespoons	Calories: 52	Protein: 1 gm	Fat Calories: 1
Total Fat: 0 gm	Dietary Fiber: 0 gm	Saturated Fat: 0 gm	Carbs: 14 gm
Sodium: 6 mg	Fat Component: 1%	Cholesterol: 0 mg	Calcium: 8 mg

Following the Guidelines of
The American Heart Association

A complete statement of the American Heart Association's Guidelines for Healthy Adults can be obtained by contacting your local chapter, or logging on to: www.americanheart.org

 For healthy adults, this cookbook presents a simple approach to following these guidelines. Keeping track of the nutritional components will help provide an understanding of your diet.

Make a habit of reaching for fruit or naturally sweetened products. The recipes in this book offer an alternative to traditional high-fat and high-calorie desserts, but they are not intended to be eaten every day or amounts greater than shown.

Keep the amount of commercially prepared foods to a minimum. Enjoy a wide variety of fresh foods that will provide a broad range of natural vitamins, minerals and nutrients. Fresh fruits and vegetables can be eaten regularly, without restriction.

Carbohydrates contribute up to 50-60% of a healthful diet. Focus on whole grain flours, seeds, nuts, legumes, beans, vegetables and fruits. The American Heart Association recommends calories be adjusted to achieve and maintain a healthy weight.

By reducing meat and chicken, a large amount of saturated fat (an artery-damaging fat) is replaced by proteins and more healthful fats. Saturated fats should be limited to 10% of calories. Animal products, including cheese, also contain cholesterol, so limit their intake.

Polyunsaturated fats (salmon, leafy vegetables and seeds) and especially omega-3 fatty acids, all have an anticlotting agent that helps to prevent heart attack and stroke. The mono-unsaturated fats in olive, canola and safflower oils will not raise damaging LDL levels.

Total fat intake should not exceed 30% of calories consumed. Even polyunsaturated and monounsaturated fats should be consumed in limited quantities, and will achieve the greatest benefit if they are replacing saturated fats presently consumed.

Sodium intake should follow the advice of your physician, or be limited to an average of 3 grams a day. Recipes in this book can be made without added salt. The desire for salty foods is acquired; you can become more sensitized to its taste by slowly reducing its use. And try sea salt; it is more flavorful and contains minerals not present in table salt.

Limit alcohol to one or two drinks per day.   And...
Exercise! It makes your body function and feel better, too.

Notes on using the
New England Seasonal Cooking Series

Each of the four books is oriented to take advantage of the freshest produce of the season, and a full variety of others that store well and are commonly available. Try to buy locally grown produce in the freshest condition possible. Local organic food not only has the best flavor and greatest amount of vitamins, but it also supports beneficial environmental practices and reduces gas emissions produced in transporting food.

Many fruits and vegetables can easily be frozen. Buy them in the peak of harvest, at their prime, when prices are at their lowest. If you continuously do this throughout the growing season, you'll always have a wonderful stock of delicious produce.

Nonfat and lowfat dairy products provide calcium, protein, vitamins and flavor, without the fat. Check labels for live pro-biotic cultures in yogurt, buttermilk and sour cream. They are strong antioxidants that help your body stay healthy.

A smidgen of oil or soft butter on a paper towel is sufficient to lightly grease pans. An aerosol pump spray can will also distribute a very thin coat of oil.

In recipes calling for a "pinch of salt" or "salt to taste," the sodium content in the nutritional analysis assumes .05 teaspoon of salt is added. If you are sodium-sensitive, beware of canned or prepared foods that sneak salt into every can, condiment and mixed herbs. Low-sodium processed tomatoes and bouillon broth are on supermarket shelves.

Preheating the oven or broiler only takes about 5 minutes.
Save electricity; don't warm appliances until just before they're needed.

Suggested Kitchen Tools and Utensils

Set of whisks in assorted sizes

Slotted spoon and spatula

Blender

Electric beaters

Nonstick skillet and frying pans in assorted sizes with lids

Oven casseroles with lids

Non-aluminum pots, pans and containers

Rolling pin

Large stainless steel bowl for mixing bread dough

Nonstick pie plates, regular and deep-dish

Stock Items

A good variety of spices, fresh fruits and vegetables

The freshest fin and shellfish you can find

Olive and canola oils (safflower can replace canola oil)

Butter (a little of the real thing can go a long way)

Unbleached flour, white whole wheat flour, and whole grain flours

Whole grain seeds, berries, nuts and legumes

Vegetable and fish bouillon cubes or powder

Canned or frozen peeled tomatoes and sauces (check sodium content)

Skim milk

Nonfat powdered milk (to enrich skim milk)

Nonfat buttermilk, yogurt and cream cheese

Nonfat evaporated milk

Lowfat cottage cheese

Lowfat and part-skim cheeses

Empirical Measurements

a pinch.................... ¹/₂₀ teaspoon

3 teaspoons............. 1 tablespoon

4 tablespoons................... ¼ cup

16 tablespoons................... 1 cup

2 cups............................ 1 pint

4 cups.......................... 1 quart

4 quarts....................... 1 gallon

8 quarts....................... 1 peck

16 ounces...................... 1 pound

8 ounces liquid................. 1 cup

1 ounce liquid.......... 2 tablespoons

Metric Conversions

¼ teaspoon..................... 1.23 ml

½ teaspoon...................... 2.5 ml

1 teaspoon........................ 5 ml

½ tablespoon................... 7.5 ml

1 tablespoon.................... 15 ml

¼ cup............................ 60 ml

½ cup........................... 120 ml

¾ cup........................... 180 ml

1 cup............................ 240 ml

2.2 pounds...................... 1 kilo

350º F................................ 175º C

Substitutions

1 tablespoon cornstarch......... 2 T. flour or 2 tsp. quick-cooking tapioca

2 teaspoons arrowroot........................... 1 tablespoon cornstarch

1 teaspoon baking powder... ¼ tsp. baking soda + ½ tsp. cream of tartar

½ cup packed brown sugar..... 2 T. molasses + ½ cup granulated sugar

¾ cup cracker crumbs.................................... 1 cup bread crumbs

1 tablespoon fresh herbs........................ 1 teaspoon dried herbs

1 small clove garlic............................. ⅛ teaspoon garlic powder

1 fresh onion............ 2 tablespoons instant minced onion, rehydrated

1 cup whole milk........... ½ cup skimmed evaporated milk + ½ cup water

1 cup buttermilk.................................... 1 cup nonfat plain yogurt

The Author's Point of View

In this increasingly busy world, time seems to get scooped away in the rapid pace of activity. Expediency can become a goal unto itself, and of course, everything has consequences. The daily routine of grocery shopping, family schedules, work, social relationships, household chores – all together form the structure of our values. Taking care of ourselves, and the miraculous planet that supports us, is a practice of awareness, choice and habit. It is also the legacy we share with every other being we meet. And perhaps, through a long chain of events, deeds also affect many people and environs we will never encounter.

I love the fact that every microbe, plant, insect, creature little and large, seemingly smart or not – is intricately enmeshed together in the same dance of life. With or without self-awareness, or maybe with a depth of appreciation I will never achieve, tens of thousands of different plants and animals exist. Some contribute to creating oxygen, filter-cleaning water, or (dare I hope) eating mosquitoes in my backyard. The vast majority of beings on my planet I cannot even name. An endless fascination with life is ours to explore. So, perhaps before spraying the insecticide that kills the ladybugs that eat the aphids (target of the poison spray), an enlightened thought (or friend) finds a way into my daily routine.

Watching how plants grow, what animals do, even taking a close look at the sediment we stand on, all foster appreciation. Having a concern for environmental implications starts with building empathy for anything we impact. Rabbits play a major role in my life. Yes, real house rabbits. They dance and shimmy with joy, run to kiss my nose then dart away to tend to important business, and even exercise wisdom in their own style. Remembering to open my heart and mind gives them the opportunity to be themselves, and I am amazed by what rabbits show me. There are probably myriad numbers of ways to be awakened and amazed each day. I'm no longer particular about the messenger, just eager to get the message.

It is my wish that this book will inspire your palate, creativity, and heart.

A northern snowshoe hare in its summer coat. Snowshoe hares inhabit northern New England, and eastern cottontails the southern half. Both benefit from the season's supply of wild apples, berries, nuts, grains, leaves, flowers and grass.

My babe, Miss Maple

Photography Copyrights and Credits

Frank Colony: page 4 Sherri and Bill Eldridge in Acadia National Park, ME.
Jim Morin (photo) and Shoals Marine Lab, Cornell University (copyright):
      page 50 Celia Thaxter's Garden, Appledore Island, Isles of Shoals, NH.
Michael Leonard: page 87 Yarmouth Clam Festival parade image, ME.
Gary Antonetti: end sheet maps.
The Harvest Hill Press logo is owned by Harvest Hill Press.

Sherri Eldridge: front cover peach pie, blueberry muffins, blueberry plants,
corn and lobster; back cover cole slaw and crab soufflé; spine blueberry plants;
back side of end sheets yellow floral pattern; page 6 sunflower; page 11 layered
compote; page 12 single raspberry; page 13 melons in basket and deer; page 23
blueberry plants; page 25 bowl of granola; page 29 muffins; page 30 all photos
in blueberry field; page 31 muffins; page 35 North shore of Great Head in Acadia
National Park; page 36 sliced bread; page 40 Bright Sunset dayliles, Siloam Double
Classic daylilies, camassia, Guernsey Cream clematis, What a Peach rose, azaleas,
Annabelle hydrangeas, Francee hosta in shade garden; page 43 bread loaf;
page 50 both crab soufflé photos; page 59 cucumber tea sandwiches; page 63
cole slaw; page 69 prepared beets; page 74 peach gelatin mold; page 83 man
processing soup in mill and bowl of soup; page 84 lobster bouillabaisse; page 101
lobster pies; page 102 lobster platter; page 103 all photos of how to eat a lobster;
page 104 fried sole and potatoes; page 115 primavera; page 122 eggplants;
page 127 baked beans; page 134 husked corn; page 144 tomatoes in basket;
page 145 sunflowers; page 147 onions; page 152 blueberry plants; page 154
peaches in bowl; page 155 sliced peaches in bowl; page 163 corn; page 164
unbaked pie and rolling pin, apple pie slice and peach pie slice; page 171 lowbush
blueberry plants; page 173 peaches; page 184 Miss Maple rabbit.

Thanks to Sanford Kelly for allowing me to photograph Rockdale Farm
in Jonesport, Maine, and for two lovely days in his wild blueberry fields.
Sanford is shown on page 30 hand-harvesting the delicate wild blueberries.

Reproduction rights for other photos and graphics were acquired as stock images.

Index

Almond Crab Soufflé 51
Antipasto, Garden Style 55
Appetizer Index 44
Apple
    Apple-Raisin Cole Slaw 63
    Apple Indian Pudding 163
    Cherry-Glazed Fruit 10
    Glazed Apple Kuchen 153
    Quick Crab Apple Bread 42
    Real Apple Butter 15
Applesauce,
    Zucchini and Everything Nice Muffins 29
Apricot
    Apricot Fruit Dip 60
    Curried Apricot Chutney 179
    Whipped Apricot Cream 9
Artichoke Florentine 141
Asparagus
    Asparagus and Crab Omelette 21
    Cream of Asparagus 83
    Quick Stir-Fry Asparagus 140
A Summer's Night Chocolate Kisses 162

Back Bay Clam Chowder 87
Baked Blueberry Porridge 23
Baked Goods Index 26
Baked Stuffed Tomatoes 129
Basil
    Pesto Guacamole 57
    Pesto Penne 118
    Tomato Basil Vinaigrette 72
Beans Index 114
    Bean-Hole Beans 128
    Boston Spirited Baked Beans 127
    Savory Succotash 135
Beets
    Carrot-Beet Julienne 131
    Creamy Beets 69
    Pickled Beets 178

Bill's Blueberry Pancakes 14
Biscuits, New London Ship's 34
Blackberry Clafouti 150
Blueberries, about 30
    Baked Blueberry Porridge 23
    Bill's Blueberry Pancakes 14
    Blueberry Maple Syrup 14
    Blueberry Muffins 31
    Blueberry Topping 166
    Machias' Best Blueberry Jam 170
    Raspberry Melon Salad 13
    Wild Blueberry Pie 152
Bluefish, Char-Blackened 99
Boston Cream Pie 156
Boston Spirited Baked Beans 127
Bouillabaisse, Northend Lobster 84
Bran, Morning Glory Muffins 28
Brandied Peach Preserves 173
Brandied Shrimp Scampi 95
Breads Index 26
Breakfast and Fruit Index 8
Broccoli with Lemon Butter 132
Broiled Oysters 49
Butterflies, about 17
Buttermilk Fan-Tans 33

Cabbage, Apple-Raisin Cole Slaw 63
Cake
    Boston Cream Pie 156
    Vermont's Finest Maple-Hazelnut Torte 160
    Portsmouth Pear Spice Cake 158
Canning Procedures 169
Cape Ann Tuna Noodle Casserole 119
Carrots
    Carrot-Beet Julienne 131
    Curried Carrot Soup 78
Cauliflower, Herbed 133
Char-Blackened Bluefish 99
Chatham Haddock Balls 52

Cheesecake, Lemon w/ Blueberry Topping 166
Cherry
    Cherry-Glazed Fruit 10
    Cheery Cherry Jam 171
    Fresh Cherry Crepes 16
Chestnut Stuffing 124
Chilled Green Beans 145
Chocolate
    A Summer's Night Chocolate Kisses 162
    Boston Cream Pie 156
    Chocolate-Pecan Oatmeal Cookies 161
    Chocolate Needham Squares 167
Chowders Index 76
Chutney, Curried Apricot 179
Cinnamon Pecan Bread 43
Clafouti, Blackberry 150
Clams, about 48
    Back Bay Clam Chowder 87
    Lobster Bake at Sunset 102
Cobbler, Peach Crumb 155
Cocktails 58
Coconut, Chocolate Needham Squares 167
Codfish Cakes 107
Cognac Creamed Crab 100
Cole Slaw, Apple-Raisin 63
Compote, Strawberry-Rhubarb 11
Cookies, Chocolate-Pecan Oatmeal 161
Connecticut 34, 35, 61, 66, 105, 126, 139,
    141, 174
Corn, about 134
    Fresh Roasted Corn 135
    Lobster Bake at Sunset 102
    Savory Succotash 135
Cornmeal
    Apple Indian Pudding 163
    Johnny Cakes 27
Crab
    Almond Crab Soufflé 51
    Asparagus and Crab Omelette 21
    Cognac Creamed Crab 100
    Crab (Lobster) Ravioli 120
    Crazy Crab Dip 56

Crab Apple, Quick Crab Apple Bread 42
Cranberry
    Quick Crab Apple Bread 42
    Zucchini and Everything Nice Muffins 29
Crazy Crab Dip 56
Cream of Asparagus 83
Creamy Beets 69
Creamy Cold Cucumber Soup 77
Crepes, Fresh Cherry Crepes 16
Crispy Breakfast Potatoes 24
Cucumber
    Creamy Cold Cucumber Soup 77
    Cucumber Finger Tea Sandwiches 59
Curried Apricot Chutney 179
Curried Carrot Soup 78

Desserts Index 148
Deviled Shrimp 46
Dill
    Smooth Yogurt-Dill Dressing 75
    Poached Salmon with Dill Sauce 109
Dips
    Apricot Fruit Dip 60
    Crazy Crab Dip 56
    Pesto Guacamole 57
Dressings
    Honey-French Dressing 75
    Smooth Yogurt-Dill Dressing 75
    Tomato Basil Vinaigrette 72
Dumplings, Vegetable Soup 81

Eggplant, Layered Eggplant Provençal 122
Eggs
    Deviled Shrimp 46
    Egg and Potato Salad 65
    Eggs Benedict Florentine 20
    Asparagus and Crab Omelette 21
Elegant Lobster Pie 101
Endive, Seared Tuna with Endive 70
Exploring New England 66

Farmers' Markets, about 144
Florentine
    Artichoke Florentine 141
    Eggs Benedict Florentine 20
    Flounder Florentine 105
Flounder Florentine 105
Flowers, about 40
Fourth of July Cherry Bombs 61
French Toast 19
Fresh Cherry Crepes 16
Fresh Greens Index 62
Fresh Lemonade Syrup 175
Fresh Roasted Corn 135
Frittata, Spinach 142
Fruit, Breakfast and Fruit Index 8

Gardens, Vegetable, about 80
    Flower, about 40
Garden Style Antipasto 55
Gazpacho, Quick 86
Gelatin, Peachy-Keen Mint Mold 74
Glazed Apple Kuchen 153
Grains Index 114
Granola, Great Granola 25
Green Beans, Chilled 145
Greens, Mixed Steamed 132
Grilling, about 98
    Char-Blackened Bluefish 99
    Skewered Braised Scallops 97

Haddock, Chatham Haddock Balls 52
Halibut with Parsley Sauce 106
Hearty Vegetable Minestrone 82
Herbed Buttermilk Bread 38
Herbed Cauliflower 133
Historic architecture, about 139
Honey-French Dressing 75
Honeynut Picnic Brown Bread 41
Hummingbirds, about 17

Italian Influence, about 116

Jams Index 168
    Cheery Cherry Jam 171
    Machias' Best Blueberry Jam 170
Jelly, Plum 172
Johnny Cakes 27
Juice, about 22

Kuchen, Glazed Apple Kuchen 153

Lasagna with Roasted Bell Peppers 117
Layered Eggplant Provençal 122
Leeks
    Marinated Lentil and Leek Salad 64
    Cream of Asparagus 83
Lemonade, Fresh Lemonade Syrup 175
Lemon Cheesecake w/ Blueberry Topping 166
Lentils
    Marinated Lentil and Leek Salad 64
    Zesty Lentil Stew 79
Lighthouses of New England 174
Lobster, about 85
    Elegant Lobster Pie 101
    How to Eat a Lobster 103
    How to Steam Lobsters 101
    Lobster Bake at Sunset 102
    Lobster Quiche Tarts 45
    Lobster Ravioli 120
    Newport Harbor Lobster Stew 93
    Northend Lobster Bouillabaisse 84

Main Meal Dishes Index 94
Maine 18, 21, 30, 35, 47, 53, 66, 68, 85, 87, 90,
    110 121, 126-128, 131, 139, 159, 167, 170, 174
Maine, Shrimp Salad 68
Maine Wild Blueberries, about 30, 170
Maple
    Blueberry Maple Syrup 14
    Vermont's Finest Maple-Hazelnut Torte 160
    Maple-Mustard Salmon 110
    Raspberry Sauce 19
Marinated Lentil and Leek Salad 64
Marine Mammals, about 53

Marmalade, Sweet Pepper 177
Martini Classic 58
Marvelous Greek Mushrooms 54
Massachusetts 27, 35, 52, 53, 61, 66, 68,
     81, 90, 97, 102, 119, 126, 134, 156, 174
Melon
     Raspberry Melon Salad 13
     Whipped Apricot Cream 9
Mixed Steamed Greens 132
Morning Glory Muffins 28
Muffins
     Blueberry Muffins 31
     Morning Glory Muffins 28
Mushrooms
     Marvelous Greek Mushrooms 54
     Mushroom Quiche 137
     Rye Berries with Mushrooms 125
Mussels, about 48
     Mussels in Vermouth Sauce 96

Nantucket Seafood Chowder 88
New England Pot Pie 112
New Hampshire 27, 35, 66, 68, 126, 127,
     128, 143, 159, 174
New London Ship's Biscuits 34
Newport Harbor Lobster Stew 93
Northend Lobster Bouillabaisse 84
North Woods Mammals, about 159

Oats
     Chocolate-Pecan Oatmeal 161
     Oatmeal Bread 39
     Great Granola 25
Omelette, Asparagus and Crab 21
Onions
     New England Pot Pie 112
     Onion Pie au Gratin 147
Oven-Fried Swordfish 111
Oysters
     Broiled Oysters 49
     Oysters, about 48
     Oyster Stew 92

Pancakes
     Bill's Blueberry Pancakes 14
     Whole Grain Hotcakes 15
Parks, New England, about 35
Party Margaritas 58
Pasta Index 114
Peaches, about 154
     Brandied Peach Preserves 173
     Peach Crumb Cobbler 155
     Peachy-Keen Mint Mold 74
Pears
     Cherry-Glazed Fruit 10
     Portsmouth Pear Spice Cake 158
Peas, Roasted Asiago Peas 138
Pecan
     Chocolate-Pecan Oatmeal 161
     Cinnamon Pecan Bread 43
     Vanilla Pecan Waffles 18
Peppers
     Lasagna w/ Roasted Bell Peppers 117
     Rainbow Pepper Pasta Salad 67
     Sweet Pepper Marmalade 177
Pesto
     Pesto Guacamole 57
     Pesto Penne 118
Pickled Beets 178
Picnics, about 90
Pies and Tarts, about 164
     Raspberry Pie 165
     Wild Blueberry Pie 152
Plums
     Plum Jelly 172
     Plums in Sweet Vermouth Sauce 151
Poached Salmon with Dill Sauce 109
Porridge, Baked Blueberry Porridge 23
Portsmouth Pear Spice Cake 158
Potatoes
     Back Bay Clam Chowder 87
     Chocolate Needham Squares 167
     Crispy Breakfast Potatoes 24
     Egg and Potato Salad 65
     Spicy Roasted Potatoes 143

Preserves Index 168
    Brandied Peach Preserves 173
    Tomato Preserves 176
Primavera, Providence Primavera 115
Puffins, about 121

Quiche
    Lobster Quiche Tarts 45
    Mushroom Quiche 137
Quick Breads
    Quick Crab Apple Bread 42
    Quick Sweet Wheat Bread 36
Quick Gazpacho 86
Quick Stir-Fry Asparagus 140

Rainbow Pepper Pasta Salad 67
Raisin
    Apple-Raisin Cole Slaw 63
    Morning Glory Muffins 28
Raspberries, about 12
    Raspberry Melon Salad 13
    Raspberry Pie 165
    Raspberry Sauce 19
Real Apple Butter 15
Red Rickey 58
Rhode Island 27, 37, 63, 66, 86, 116, 126,
    139, 146, 174
Rhubarb, Strawberry-Rhubarb Compote 11
Risotto, Zucchini and Shrimp Risotto 123
Roasted Asiago Peas 138
Rolls
    Buttermilk Fan-Tans 33
    New London Ship's Biscuits 34
    Sourdough Dough Rye Rolls 32
Romaine, Robust Salad 72
Rutabaga Mash 146
Rye, Sourdough Rye Rolls 32
Rye Berries with Mushrooms 125

Sailing, about 90
Salads Index 62

Salmon, about 108
    Maple-Mustard Salmon 110
    Poached Salmon with Dill Sauce 109
    Smoked Salmon Toasts 50
Sandwiches, Cucumber Finger Teas 59
Sangria Pitcher Party 58
Savory Succotash 135
Scallops
    Nantucket Seafood Chowder 88
    Seafood Newburg 113
    Skewered Braised Scallops 97
Scampi, Brandied Shrimp Scampi 95
Seafood
    Nantucket Seafood Chowder 88
    New England Pot Pie 112
    Seafood Newburg 113
    Zuppa di Pesca 91
Seared Tuna with Endive 70
Shrimp, about 68
    Brandied Shrimp Scampi 95
    Deviled Shrimp 46
    Maine Shrimp Salad 68
    Nantucket Seafood Chowder 88
    Shrimp (Lobster) Ravioli 120
    Shrimp Bisque 89
    Zucchini and Shrimp Risotto 123
Simply Sole 104
Skewered Braised Scallops 97
Smoked Salmon Toasts 50
Smooth Yogurt-Dill Dressing 75
Sole, Simply Sole 104
Sorbet, White Grape Sorbet 157
Soufflé, Almond Crab Soufflé 51
Soups and Stews Index 76
Sourdough Rye Rolls 32
Spicy Roasted Potatoes 143
Spinach
    Artichoke Florentine 141
    Eggs Benedict Florentine 20
    Flounder Florentine 105
    Spinach and Pine Nut Salad 71
    Spinach Frittata 142

Strawberry
    Strawberry-Rhubarb Compote 11
    Strawberry Crisp 149
    Strawberry Daiquiri 58
Strudel, Vegetable Strudel 47
Succotash, Savory Succotash 135
Sweet Pepper Marmalade 177
Swordfish, Oven-Fried 111
Syrup
    Blueberry Maple Syrup 14
    Raspberry Sauce 19

Tarts, about 164
    Lobster Quiche Tarts 45
Toasting White Bread 37
Tomato, about 73
    Baked Stuffed Tomatoes 129
    Fourth of July Cherry Bombs 61
    Tomato Basil Vinaigrette 72
    Tomato Preserves 176
Toppings
    Blueberry Maple Syrup 14
    Blueberry Topping 166
    Raspberry Sauce 19
    Real Apple Butter 15
Torte, Vermont's Finest Maple-Hazelnut 160
Tuna
    Cape Ann Tuna Noodle Casserole 119
    Char-Blackened Bluefish 99
    Seared Tuna with Endive 70
Turnip, Rutabaga Mash 146

Vanilla Pecan Waffles 18
Vegetables, Mixed
    Garden Style Antipasto 55
    Hearty Vegetable Minestrone 82
    New England Pot Pie 112
    Providence Primavera 115
    Quick Gazpacho 86
    Vegetable Soup with Dumplings 81
    Vegetable Strudel 47
    Zesty Lentil Stew 79

Vegetables and Sauces Index 130
Vegetable Soup with Dumplings 81
Vermont 35, 66, 90, 126, 127, 136, 139,
    150, 159, 170, 174
Vineyards and Wines, about 126

Waffles, Vanilla Pecan Waffles 18
Wheat, Quick Sweet Wheat Bread 36
Whipped Apricot Cream 9
White Grape Sorbet 157
Whole Grains
    Baked Blueberry Porridge 23
    Baked Stuffed Tomatoes 129
    Cooking grain berries 23
    Great Granola 25
    Morning Glory Muffins 28
    Rye Berries with Mushrooms 125
    Whole Grain Hotcakes 15
Wild Blueberries, about 30
    Wild Blueberry Pie 152
Windmills, about 27
Wines, about 126

Yeast Breads
    Buttermilk Fan-Tans 33
    Cinnamon Pecan Bread 43
    Herbed Buttermilk Bread 38
    Honeynut Picnic Brown Bread 41
    Oatmeal Bread 39
    Sourdough Rye Rolls 32
    Toasting White Bread 37
Yogurt
    Smooth Yogurt-Dill Dressing 75
    Whipped Apricot Cream 9

Zesty Lentil Stew 79
Zucchini
    Zucchini and Everything Nice Muffins 29
    Zucchini and Shrimp Risotto 123
    Zucchini Hash Browns 136
Zuppa di Pesca 91

If you enjoy this summertime cookbook, please watch for publication of the other three seasonal cookbooks in 2007 and 2008. Each cookbook has 150 lowfat recipes, and extends the photographic journey through the regional beauty, history and culinary culture of New England. Cookbooks are also a lovely gift that will be used for years to come.

New England Spring Cooking
New England Summertime Cooking
New England Fall Harvest Cooking
New England Winterfare Cooking

Cookbooks can be ordered on our website, by mail or phone at:
www.harvesthillpress.com
Harvest Hill Press
P.O. Box 55
Salisbury Cove, Maine 04672
207-288-8900

Cost per book is $19.95.
Shipping cost is $5.00 per order (any quantity) to one U.S. address.
Maine residents add 5% sales tax.

VISA and MasterCard orders ship in 3 days.
Please include cardholder name, card number and expiry date.

Orders with check payable to Harvest Hill Press ship in 3 weeks.

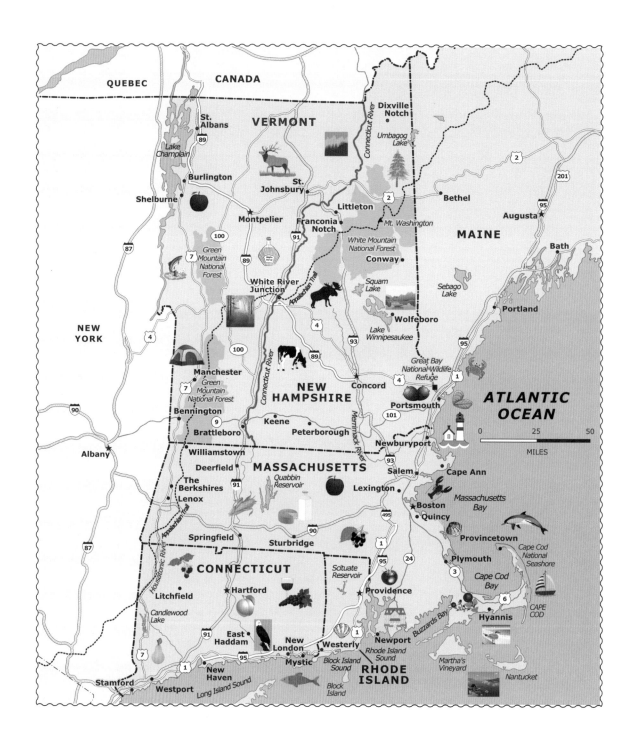

QUEBEC

CANADA

NEW YORK

VERMONT

St. Albans

89

Lake Champlain

Burlington

Shelburne

Montpelier

100

7

Green Mountain National Forest

89

White River Junction

St. Johnsbury

Franconia Notch

91

Littleton

Dixville Notch

Connecticut River

Umbagog Lake

2

Bethel

Mt. Washington

White Mountain National Forest

Conway

Squam Lake

MAINE

95

Augusta

201

2

Bath

Sebago Lake

Portland

NEW YORK

4

Appalachian Trail

4

Wolfeboro

Lake Winnipesaukee

95

Great Bay National Wildlife Refuge

100

Manchester

Green Mountain National Forest

7

89

NEW HAMPSHIRE

Concord

1

ATLANTIC OCEAN

90

Bennington

9

Keene

Portsmouth

101

Merrimack River

Connecticut River

Brattleboro

Peterborough

Newburyport

Albany

Williamstown

Deerfield

MASSACHUSETTS

93

Salem

Cape Ann

0   25   50

MILES

The Berkshires

Lenox

91

Quabbin Reservoir

Lexington

Boston

Quincy

Massachusetts Bay

495

Springfield

90

Sturbridge

1

Provincetown

Cape Cod National Seashore

87

Appalachian Trail

Housatonic River

CONNECTICUT

Scituate Reservoir

95

24

Plymouth

3

Cape Cod Bay

6

CAPE COD

Litchfield

Hartford

Providence

Hyannis

Candlewood Lake

91

East Haddam

New London

Westerly

1

Newport

Buzzards Bay

7

95

Mystic

Block Island Sound

Rhode Island Sound

RHODE ISLAND

Martha's Vineyard

Nantucket

Stamford

Westport

New Haven

1

Long Island Sound

Block Island